BLESSED  NESS

Finding Peace in the Challenges

of Aging and Illness

BLESSED BY OUR BROKENNESS

Finding Peace in the Challenges of Aging and Illness

Anne Field, OSB

The Word Among Us Press
9639 Doctor Perry Road
Ijamsville, Maryland 21754
www.wordamongus.org

11 10 09 08   2 3 4 5
ISBN: 978-1-59325-111-6

Cover design by John Hamilton Design

Library of Congress Cataloging-in-Publication Data
Field, Anne, 1924-
    Blessed by our brokenness : finding peace in the challenges of aging and
illness / Anne Field.
       p. cm.
    Includes bibliographical references.
    ISBN 978-1-59325-111-6 (alk. paper)
    1. Suffering--Religious aspects--Christianity. 2. Aging--Religious aspects-
-Christianity. I. Title.
    BV4909.F54 2007
    248.8'6--dc22
                                    2007032149

CONTENTS

A thorn was given me in the flesh, a messenger of Satan to torment me, to keep me from being too elated. Three times I appealed to the Lord about this, that it would leave me, but he said to me, "My grace is sufficient for you, for power is made perfect in weakness."

—2 Corinthians 12:7-9

Chapter One

Why Does God Allow Such Things?

*We know that all things work together
for good for those who love God, who are
called according to his purpose.*

—Romans 8:28

It is a rare day that we do not see several messages posted on our community bulletin board from people—both known and unknown to us—pleading for prayers for themselves or their loved ones. Many are suffering from the cruel blows of an apparently mindless fate that has deprived them of the fullness of life and well-being that was their birthright. A devastating stroke, the discovery of cancer, an accident that results in paralysis, an insidious disease, a virulent infection—all these not only shock and grieve us but also strike fear into our hearts. They make us painfully aware of our own vulnerability and the fragility of all flesh. There is so much suffering all around us, senseless and pointless in itself. Does it have any meaning at all?

These thoughts were first sown in my mind by Alice, a resident of our village who used to attend Sunday Mass in the abbey church. Though I didn't know her personally, I was concerned when I saw her being brought to the visitors' chapel in a wheelchair. I soon learned that she had undergone surgery for a hip replacement, which had not been successful. She was permanently disabled and in great pain. Some time later, her husband brought her to the Halloween social we celebrate each year with the local people who worship with us, and I had an opportunity to talk with her. It had not been very long since my own hip replacement surgery, which had not been entirely successful either, so I felt a certain affinity with Alice and looked forward to sharing our experiences.

However, to my dismay, I found her totally embittered. She would accept nothing I said and seemed determined not to be helped. All she could talk about was suing the National Health Service for compensation. Since she had been provided with a wheelchair and every other available aid, there seemed to be nothing more that compensation could have obtained for her, except perhaps the satisfaction of making the Health Service pay. Whether she did in fact file the lawsuit I never heard, but I was told that she made life so intolerable for her family that they finally placed her in a nursing home. When she died a few years later, I grieved for her, praying that at the end she had found serenity and peace with God.

After Alice's death, I continued to think about her. Isn't there something positive that people can discover in the diminishments and disabilities that lie in wait for them, whether from aging, illness, or from our accident-prone world? Could these challenges possibly become a source of grace and help us grow to our full spiritual stature?

Not a few people think that only the bad things are God's will and that any good things happen in spite of it. When people suffer any diminishments or disabilities in their lives, well-meaning friends often tell them that it is God's will and they must be resigned to it. They may not go as far as Job's friends, who tried to convince him that he was being punished for his sins; yet, it is clear that in their view, God's will is equated with suffering. Whatever led them to have such a poor opinion of their heavenly Father?

On the contrary, I believe that what happens to us is not necessarily God's special visitation or a spiteful whim of fate; it is simply raw material. It comes from God in the sense that nothing can happen outside of his providence. But we live in an evolving, experimenting, clashing universe that sometimes throws us delights, sometimes horrors. Our environment can be breathtaking in its beauty, yet it is liable to cast up mutations and bacilli that unintentionally wreak havoc. As the created universe hurtles forward in time and space from the simple elements of its beginning to life as we now know and experience it, many are the accidents along the way.

Seizing the Opportunity

Yet this raw material is our opportunity for growth and self-transcendence, capable of becoming an immense grace for us. In the words of Scripture, the whole of creation can be said to be waiting with eager longing to see if we seize the opportunity and achieve the freedom of the children of God (see Romans 8:19-21). Some things are beyond our control. Others are, at all times, within our control, such as the spiritual response we make to situations in which the Lord is pleased to put us and the determination to find God in all the circumstances of our lives—joys or sorrows. These situations and circumstances present us with a challenge. Life can be unfair, often cruel, always uncertain, offering no security. Yet this is the context of our task in this world.

Some things are the outcome of human malice and the mystery of sin and evil. God took a great risk in giving us free will. Even without deliberate intent to harm, some of the bad things that happen are due to human selfishness, carelessness, or clumsiness. But even these can be utilized for good in unexpected ways. Marvelous acts of compassion and assistance were witnessed after the terrorist attacks of September 11, 2001. Help was offered by many people who, before that unforgettable day, had given little thought to the needs of others outside their own world. How many people who may have grown listless and slothful about doing good have once again found the will to reach out to others in need?

The horrors of the wartime concentration camps gave rise to acts of immense love, and those who survived learned the all-important lesson that the strongest force in the world is love. They discovered that what kept the spark of humanity alive was compassion for others. As Jean Daniélou wrote in *The Lord of History,* what counts in the end is our response to circumstances, not the circumstances themselves, which have neither value nor demerit of their own.[1] Adversity itself can be a creative force that calls forth a response from the depths of our souls, whereas prosperity often leaves people content with the surface of life as they find it.

A Mystery That Demands Faith

Some of the hardest trials to bear are the loss of our faculties—when our hearing, sight, and mobility are impaired, our memory lets us down, our skills desert us, or our health and strength deteriorate. Sometimes disabilities are simply part of the aging process. But sometimes people are struck down by accident or illness while they are still in the prime of life. How many promising careers and endeavors can be abruptly cut short! How difficult it is to see God's providence in such events! When adversity strikes us, our instinctive response is "Why me? What have I done to deserve this? How can I believe in an all-powerful, loving God who lets such things happen?"

These questions have been asked throughout human history. Theologians have proposed solutions that, although true, rarely convince the sufferer. This is because evil and suffering are part of a mystery that demands faith—the kind of faith that Jesus sought from those who asked him for healing during his public ministry. It demands a faith that is equated to trust in God's goodness and promises simply because he is a God of mercy and compassion. It was never God's predetermined will that his creatures should suffer. "God did not make death, and he does not delight in the death of the living. For he created all things so that they might exist" (Wisdom 1:13-14). But having given free will to human beings, he allowed their choices to initiate consequences not directly of their choosing, and he showed his almighty power in turning those consequences to their ultimate good—though not without their acceptance and cooperation. Were he to prevent our actions from proceeding to their conclusions, he would be limiting our free will and would, in effect, be treating us like puppets.

We can see this truth illustrated in the story of Adam and Eve. Scripture shows how Adam and Eve were tempted and fell, how they knew shame and guilt, how they tried to hide from God, and how they made excuses and tried to pass on the blame. We see God listening to their sorry tale and pronouncing on them the sentence their disobedience had incurred. People might ask, If God loved Adam and Eve so much, couldn't he have stopped them from eating the forbidden fruit? Yet that was not God's way. Having given them free will, he allowed them to choose for themselves, knowing they would choose what was not good for them and what would be harmful to others. But it was also in his power to send them, in the fullness of time, a salvation more glorious than all they had lost. Even in their fall, God never ceased to love them. After their sin and condemnation, Scripture gives us the touching account of God's solicitude for them in their nakedness: he made them clothing of skins (see Genesis 3:21)! This unexpected detail in the Genesis story makes us smile. But it is the inspired writer's way of showing us how we, who also try to hide from God after we have done wrong because we feel sure he no longer loves us, can be convinced that the God who is Love is never deterred from caring for what he has made.

Chapter 1

A New Task and Treasure

So, when we suffer diminishments or losses, the response
God's will be done, which our friends may piously urge us
to make, does not mean we should adopt a defeatist attitude
toward our fate, a refusal of hope. It means a willing acceptance of what is as yet hidden from our sight: the infinitely
resourceful wisdom and love of a God who is able to turn
all things to the good of those who love him (see Romans
8:28). If our faculties are impaired or even destroyed, it is
not something God does to punish us or even, I think, a
predetermined means of instructing us. It gives him no pleasure to see his creation marred. But it does give him great
joy to see us courageously facing up to the challenge of our
loss, striving with all our strength and ingenuity to overcome it, and discovering in what is physically irremediable
an inner, secret mode of perception and working. Though
the future is unknown to us and the scope of our lives and
work diminished in painful ways not of our choosing, our
faith in God's power to turn it all to good need not be limited to the heaven we hope for beyond the grave. The disabilities from which we suffer may even now offer us a new
task and treasure in this life, and our outward limitations
reveal to us an inner landscape we might never otherwise
have explored.

The loss of faculties can also open us to the world of the
disabled. Each diminishment offers us an entrance through
a new door of experience and empathy. We are invited to

enter freely and walk resolutely through successive doors, confident that God will give us new blessings, new ministries. We can identify with all who endure these diminishments, embracing and comforting them in the compassionate heart of Jesus. By our intercession, we can bring them all to Christ dwelling within us. God does not provide the answers to our problems; instead, he enters with us into the questions. While the media are interested only in the bad news and ignore the good, with God's help we shall find unexpected meaning in what is, in and of itself, meaningless.

In what follows, I hope to explore some of the possibilities these diminishments may have to offer us and ponder some of the ways in which we can befriend them and turn them into blessings.

1. Jean Daniélou, *The Lord of History: Reflections on the Inner Meaning of History* (London: Henry Regnery Co., 1958).

Chapter Two

THE INNER JOURNEY

*I will lead the blind by a road they do not know,
by paths they have not known
I will guide them.*

—Isaiah 42:16

We all take our faculties for granted until we lose them, and unfortunately, it is after we lose them that we realize what wonderful gifts they were, how perfectly designed to do exactly what was required of them. I never knew, for instance, that I possessed a muscle that took charge of transferring my weight from one leg to the other as I walked. Only when this abductor muscle was rendered permanently useless—by accidental damage during hip replacement surgery—did I realize how perfectly it had functioned before.

In my childhood, I loved walking in the gentle, pleasant lanes and woods surrounding my home and learning to recognize the abundant indigenous flora and fauna in the area. Later, in our monastery enclosure, I studied birds and their songs and herbs with their healing properties. It was a great and unfailing joy to see how God had filled the earth not only with beauty but also with plants that promote health. I became a keen gardener. I grew medicinal and aromatic herbs, harvesting and drying them to make teas, infusions, and ointments and blending them for use in fragrant, sleep-inducing pillows and soothing lotions. My hobby became a small industry; visitors eagerly purchased these items in the abbey shop and were greatly disappointed when new assignments forced me to stop making them.

I was then put in charge of creating a flower garden at the monastery guesthouse. I studied garden designs and growth patterns, planned color schemes, and learned pruning and propagating skills. I dug, sowed, and planted, and I talked encouragingly to the reluctant beauties among my flowers to coax them into bloom, as recommended by garden enthusiasts. Again I found much joy in the task, for gardeners are most often happy people who feel privileged to share God's work of creation.

Gardening is an occupation that brings many friends— gardeners themselves, who enjoy exchanging seedlings and cuttings and discussing plants and growing techniques, or simply people who love the beauty of flowers and trees, and the opportunity of relaxing among them.

Some of our guests were elderly and infirm, and I came to love them in a special way because of their courage and interest in all they saw. They taught me much as I struggled with my own increasing locomotive difficulties. After it became clear that I would always be disabled, the National Health Service provided me with an electric wheelchair. I would never have presumed to ask for one, but the chair made it so much easier for me to get to church for our community's prayer and liturgy, as well as to the library some distance away. It also meant that I could still get to the guesthouse garden. Since the buildings at our monastery are registered as historical sites and so have no disability access, we bought a pair of portable ramps. I would cautiously ride down these ramps in my chair and then around the house in order to reach the postern gate. The drive, courtyard, and paths at the guesthouse were nearly all paved, so it was much easier than bumping around the orchard inside the enclosure—although in summer when the ground was baked hard enough, I could ride across the lawn and grassy field to a spot overlooking the monastery pond, with its moorhens and ducks. But St. Mary's guesthouse was my usual objective.

Frequently there would be guests with similar disabilities; we quickly became friends. How often I was humbled by their courage, especially of those who lived alone! And what enjoyment we experienced exchanging tips about ways of coping. So many of them were far worse off than I. We came to understand that although for us physical travels were no longer on the agenda, there is an *inner* journey to be explored.

Our Father Is the Goal of Our Journey; Jesus Is Our Way

This inner journey is the theme of *The Diving Bell and the Butterfly* by the French writer Jean-Dominique Bauby,[1] who with patient perseverance had dictated his book by blinking his left eyelid—the only movement he could still make after a devastating stroke. In his imagination, he undertook prodigious tasks and journeys: he conducted orchestras; painted masterpieces; became a famous athlete, mountaineer, explorer, astronaut, surgeon, professor, inventor, musician, and actor; and traveled to all parts of the world, reveling in sunny climates and the conquest of the most difficult terrains on earth. Previously, he had been an enterprising businessman, full of drive and ideas, an educated man with a well-stocked, cultivated mind, which kept him in good stead as he lay physically immobilized for the rest of his life. Now he made the most of the one gift that remained to him.

Bauby's book is an impressive testament to the capacity of the human spirit to rise above physical limitations. His was not a retreat into the past, but a constant expansion of mental horizons. He is not a particularly religious writer, but he shows us dimensions of the mind that still invite exploration—even when one is physically incapacitated. As the seventeenth-century poet Thomas Traherne wrote in his *Centuries of Meditations*, "God made you able to create worlds in your own mind which are more precious to him than those He Himself created."[2]

It is good to have a fund of inner resources like these to draw upon in challenging times: to have formed habits of worthwhile reading and study, to have learned the art of pondering the mysteries of things, and to have desired to know their Maker.

The loss of physical mobility can also be a signal that the Holy Spirit is inviting us to embark on an inner journey of faith. When we are whole, we can fail to grasp the truth of our mortality, seeing everything in the light of this life only. Disabilities are God's way of changing our sights. They challenge us to see things in the light of our eternal destiny.

For, as St. Paul says, "If for this life only we have hoped in Christ, we are of all people most to be pitied" (1 Corinthians 15:19). The things of this world will pass away, and we must set our hearts on true joys. Diminishments can be a sign that it is time for us to leave the familiar sheepfold and follow the Good Shepherd, who calls his sheep one by one and leads them out. They follow because they know his voice. Then he goes ahead of them and leads them to fresh pastures (see John 10:1-18).

In a famous sermon based on this passage from John's gospel, St. Gregory the Great urges his people to seek eagerly for the fresh grazing grounds to which the Good Shepherd is leading them, and to follow him toward the green pastures of paradise, where the saints see God face to face. There is no greater happiness than this, St. Gregory says, and no misfortune should distract us from striving toward it; for if anyone is anxious to reach a particular destination, he will not be discouraged by the roughness of the road. Neither must we allow ourselves to be diverted by the charms of prosperity, for only a foolish traveler, seeing pleasant fields along the way, will forget to go on toward his destination.[3]

The fourteenth-century English spiritual writer Walter Hilton must have known this passage well, for it has always been read in the Divine Office on Good Shepherd Sunday, now the Fourth Sunday of Easter. Hilton's book *The Ladder of Perfection* addresses our search for God, who alone can satisfy all the needs and longings of the human heart.

It contains an equally famous passage, the parable of a pilgrim who wished to go to Jerusalem. Seeking the advice of a trusted counselor, the pilgrim is told that he must set his heart wholly on reaching Jerusalem and on nothing else. In other words, said his counselor,

> Set yourself wholly on obtaining the love of Jesus, for it is to this end that you have been created and redeemed; this is your beginning and your end, your joy and your bliss. Therefore whatever you may possess and however fruitful your activities, regard them all as worthless without the inward certainty and experience of this love. Keep this intention constantly in mind and hold to it firmly; it will sustain you among all the perils of your pilgrimage. It will protect you from thieves and robbers, for although they may rob and assault you with different temptations, your life will always be safe. Your enemies will set themselves to obstruct you if they can. Nothing distresses them more than your desire and longing for the love of Jesus, and their whole purpose is to uproot this from your heart, and turn you back again to the love of earthly things. But you have one remedy. Whatever they say, do not believe them; keep on your way and let your answer always be, "I am nothing, I have nothing, I desire nothing but the love of Jesus."
>
> So long as you are on the road your enemies will not cease to harass you; at one time they will intimidate

and threaten you, at another they will try to flatter and seduce you, to make you abandon your purpose and turn back. Hold firmly to your desire and reply always that you desire to have Jesus and be at Jerusalem. They will realize that you are so determined that you will not yield to sin or illness, delusions, fits, doubts, temptations, hardships or poverty, life or death. You want one thing only, so turn a deaf ear to all their suggestions. . . . Fix your thoughts on Jesus, and do not allow any tumble to disturb you or occupy your attention. Remember what you have learned: you are nothing, you have nothing, and loss of worldly goods is nothing, for you desire nothing but the love of Jesus. If your own frailty causes you to be harassed by the troubles that beset this mortal life, regain your peace of mind as soon as possible. Do not allow your enemies to have the advantage by brooding over your difficulties. Focus your mind on this desire, strengthen and maintain it by prayer; never let it go, and it will lead you on the right road and preserve you in all dangers.[4]

This passage underscores the need for resolution and a real commitment in our lives. The Scriptures tell us, "When the days drew near for [Jesus] to be taken up, he set his face to go to Jerusalem" (Luke 9:51), and "for the sake of the joy that was set before him [he] endured the cross, disregarding its shame" (Hebrews 12:2). For our goal we are given that wonderful text in John's gospel, "And this is eternal life, that they may know you, the only true God, and Jesus Christ whom you have sent" (17:3). And again, Jesus says, "I am the way, and the truth, and the life. No one comes to the Father except through me" (14:6). To go to the Father: that is our goal, and Jesus is the way. Our journey now is an inward one, since all our other ways and goals are being taken from us. All the more, then, can we know that he is the way that leads us to the Father. If our bodies seem to be falling into decay, we know that our essential personhood is in the heart, and in the strength of our heart's desire we press ahead every day to meet the One who is waiting to take us home.

1. Jean-Dominique Bauby, *The Diving Bell and the Butterfly* (New York: Vintage Books, 1998).

2. Thomas Traherne, *Centuries of Meditations: The Second Century,* 90, ed. Bertram Dobell (London: 1908), http://www .spiritofprayer.com/00introcenturies.php.

3. St. Gregory, Homily 14:3-6.

4. Walter Hilton, *The Ladder of Perfection,* trans. Leo Sherley-Price (New York: Penguin Classics, reissue edition 1988).

Chapter Three

GOD SPEAKS TO US IN MANY WAYS

I came that they may have life,
and have it abundantly.

—John 10:10

I once came across a book describing the senses of deep-sea creatures that never see daylight. Some of them have rows of lights like portholes along their flanks to enable them to see both prey and predators; others create a chemical reaction in their bodies to produce bioluminescent light. It was clear that every animal is endowed with the senses it needs for survival and the instinctive skills to use them competently.

We humans, having developed large and complex brains, depend less on instinct than on invention and planning, although we still retain certain primitive reflexes that protect us from danger. But like the other animals, we have been given senses perfectly tailored to our needs. Our five sense organs are all wonderfully designed and precisely constructed, and they work together to enable us to live our lives to the full, as God meant them to be lived. We take these senses for granted, of course, and perhaps it is right that we should, for we most often need to focus on what the senses impart to us rather than how they work. But in this pressured and highly technological age, we often fail to draw from our sense perceptions the full riches they offer to us.

Healing through the Doorway of Our Senses

When difficulties overwhelm us and we suffer from nervous tension and insomnia, healing can often come through the doorway of the senses. What we need at these times is contact with objective reality—not the waves of depression, fear, and anxiety that go round and round our heads and focus us more often on past actions or future contingencies than on present actuality. It is through our God-given senses that we can become receptive to what is being offered by the present moment. God is always in the present. This means that contact with the "now" of the present moment is actual contact with God and his healing love.

How often do we, as Isaiah says, see without seeing and hear without hearing (6:9)? In my bird-watching days, people sometimes asked me to take them for a walk in order to point out the different birds and alert them to their songs. But when I did so, they often seemed neither to look nor to listen, making so much noise that they frightened the wild creatures away.

Instead, we must allow ourselves to become completely receptive to sounds, colors, patterns, scents, warmth and coolness—everything in creation and in art that presents itself to our sight, hearing, smell, taste, and touch. Then we can drink in the reality that alone gives nourishment to the brain and hence to our work and thought. If possible, go out into the garden, countryside, or seashore at these times; sit or stand quietly and simply see what is there. Listen attentively to the sounds of birds, insects, waves. Feel the texture of tree trunks, leaves, flowers, stones. See the patterns in clouds, in the interstices between branches, in the markings of pebbles. Inhale the scent of seaweed, or of flowers, grass mowings, or the crushed leaves of aromatic plants. Count the petals of flowers or examine the spiral patterns of pinecones or seed heads, and perhaps they will disclose some of those mysterious sequences that have been discovered in the numbers of things. Whether indoors or out, observe the shapes of tables and chairs and the proportions of buildings. Note the rhythm of machines or human bodies; see with an artist's eye the colors, shadows, reflections, and scale of objects. Even rubbish dumps, old cars, or other unlikely sights can contain unexpected visual interest. Take them into your conscious mind, and for each of these things, thank the God and Father of us all.

Deaf People Can Become a Presence of Peace

But what happens when we are deprived of one of our senses? Of our five senses, perhaps we prize sight most of all. Yet a friend who has only peripheral vision and cannot read told me that in spite of this deprivation, he much preferred being blind to being deaf, because, he said, the blind tend to attract more sympathy and consideration. This is very true, as the deaf will acknowledge. Being blind, carrying a white cane, and needing a guiding companion or dog is much more noticeable to others and so invites more kindly help and concern. My friend also pointed out how lucky we are to live today, when we can get talking books and publications in Braille, postage free, and have access to the radio—aids unknown to earlier generations. Cataracts, too, are less of a life sentence these days since they can be treated with excellent results.

But it is a different story with a hearing impairment, and many will tell you that this disability is a greater trial than the loss of any other sense. It was quite a while before I became aware of having a hearing loss. In my earlier years, I had been an avid birder, finding great joy in observing which birds frequented our monastic grounds and identifying their individual songs. It was my ambition to know all our resident species and seasonal migrants, with their songs and call notes. Though my eyesight was never particularly keen, I prided myself on acuteness of hearing, and only as I grew older did I realize that a lack of clarity in voices was more likely to be due to my reception rather than their transmission.

This problem was particularly noticeable in a crowded room where many conversations and lively discussions were being carried on simultaneously. So I applied for an audiology test and was given a hearing aid. This device was excellent in church and other places where a loop system was installed (at least when people remembered to switch it on and to use the microphone), but for general conversation it was very little help, since turning up the volume turned up background noise as well as the voices. Those with impaired hearing miss a good deal.

I thought it might help to be able to read lips, and I decided to obtain a video with an accompanying course of lessons. The lessons were very helpful, but it became evident that even after they have been mastered, a lot of hard work remains. The listener must practice great discernment, since many consonants and vowels have similar lip formations, and only by the context can one understand correctly. A great deal also depends on the consideration shown to the hard of hearing; speakers must, for example, let their mouths be clearly seen—if possible with their faces toward the light—and they must enunciate distinctly. How exasperating it can be when people speak with their faces turned away or with their hands covering their mouths! Acoustics are seldom ideal, and arguments can become lively. People interrupt one another or several speak at once. In our community discussions, speakers are encouraged to use the microphone so that the loop system can function, but in animated debates, this restraint can be forgotten.

Deafness is a handicap that normally does not elicit a lot of sympathy. The deaf can appear to be stupid or senile and are often simply left out of things. People are busy, with little time, and so those with hearing losses are often reluctant to ask others to repeat what they have just said and consequently miss out on much of what is going on. Not only can this cause a loss of confidence, it can also result in much frustration and resentment at the lack of consideration shown, though it is never intended—it is simply thoughtlessness.

Thus impaired hearing can bring increasing loneliness to many of us. But need it be so? Could it not rather be an invitation to enter into the silence of the heart and hear what the Lord God will speak, for he will speak peace to his people, to those who turn to him in their hearts (see Psalm 85:8)? When we learn to listen to the voice of God within us, we can even be thankful that it is not drowned out by the din of this world.

God speaks to us in many ways, but how often do we listen to what he is saying? There is a prayer of quiet listening, when we simply ask the Lord to tell us what we need to know and then become very still and attentive to him. His word can come in different ways, through Scripture, through other people, through events, and also through the impression on our minds of whatever he is asking of us. If this is not always a peaceful experience, it is because what he asks is contrary to our natural inclinations. For example, it took me two years to relinquish my own plans and accept his invitation to follow him in the monastic way of life—two years of kicking against the goad. I remember well the peace that flooded me when at last I surrendered. The consequence of this quiet, attentive prayer is an immersion in God's presence, which leads to a deep calm that no surface turmoil or external clamor can disturb.

When it is impossible to distinguish what is said in meetings or discussions, the deaf learn to be a simple presence, a presence of peace in the midst of argument, and to pray for both speakers and hearers and the calming of any stress that may arise. The much-loved St. Seraphim of Sarov used to tell his disciples, "Acquire a peaceful spirit, and around you thousands will be saved."[1] We can determine never to speak against opponents or enemies in a hostile way, but rather to invoke Christ's peace on all and to work for the establishment of his kingdom in our hearts, praying that he will use our hearts as "outposts" where he, the Prince of Peace, can reign.

The Blind Can See with an Inner Vision

Of course, the loss of sight is indeed a major diminishment as well. Perhaps more than any other, it closes doors to cherished dreams and ambitions, and turns to bewilderment and frustration the work we had regarded as our vocation. The poet John Milton's bitter battle against his affliction is illustrated in one of his poems:

When I consider how my light is spent
Ere half my days, in this dark world and wide,
And that one talent which is death to hide
Lodged with me useless, though my soul more bent
To serve therewith my Maker, and present
My true account, lest He returning chide,—
Doth God exact day labour, light denied?

So few lines encompass so much anguish and struggle! Yet the last two stanzas give us a glimpse of the answering calm he was eventually granted:

But Patience, to prevent
That murmur, soon replies: God doth not need

Either man's work or his own gifts: who best
Bear His mild yoke, they serve him best. His state
Is kingly; thousands at His bidding speed
And post o'er land and ocean, without rest.
They also serve who only stand and wait.[2]

Does God repent of his gifts? Or are we invited to discover a new way toward even greater creativity in the inte-
riority we are led to explore? The memories we retain of
things once seen can still be re-created in our minds, as
William Wordsworth knew when he wrote of his recollec-
tion of the sight of daffodils:

Ten thousand saw I at a glance,
Tossing their heads in sprightly dance.
The waves beside them danced; but they
Out-did the sparkling waves in glee;
A poet could not but be gay
In such a jocund company.
I gazed and gazed, but little thought
What wealth the show to me had brought:
For oft, when on my couch I lie
In vacant or in pensive mood,
They flash upon that inward eye
Which is the bliss of solitude;
And then my heart with pleasure fills,
And dances with the daffodils.[3]

Like Jean-Dominique Bauby immobilized in his hospital bed, some blind people have produced an amazing amount of literature, philosophy, and works in many other fields. I read of a poet who, after losing his sight in World War II, composed whole poems in his mind, honing and perfecting them all in his head, then dictating the finished work into a tape recorder to be typed out by an assistant. He did this work at night, since day and night were all one and the same to him, and in the night hours he was less likely to be disturbed. He was, in any case, spared the distractions and allurements that advertisements and entertainments constantly throw in our line of vision. Even so, could a sighted person have reached such a remarkable achievement? The blind learn to see with their inner eye.

I remember well an old nun of our community who went blind soon after her solemn profession. I knew her as a truly joy-filled person. She had developed many practical skills throughout her life; for example, she looked after the poultry, rang the bells, wove baskets, and even typed documents. Over the years, she was able to say from her heart that she no longer wished to have her sight restored in this life, because the next face she would see would be the face of Christ. Always alert and active in hope, death had no fears for her. She was a powerful witness to the unseen presence of Christ in her heart.

Recently a woman in her early fifties stayed at our guesthouse during Holy Week and Easter. She had been blind since the age of four, but she, too, gave me the impression of great joy and enthusiasm for life. With the help of a guide dog, she was able to live independently and travel as she wished. I was greatly impressed by the confidence with which she tripped lightly up and down steps and negotiated doors and passages. She was fortunate enough to have a good job at a neurological institute typing reports on a special word processor that had the capacity to turn her typing into speech and play it back to her as she worked. Printed pages could also be translated into speech. The documents she produced offered the additional bonus of being both interesting and educational in themselves as well as of value to the medical field. Of course, as my friend remarked, we are very lucky to be living in an age when technology offers so much assistance to the blind.

But our guest told me that even if she were offered a new kind of surgery to restore her sight, she would not accept it because of the benefits she has gained. Her hearing, she said, had been enhanced by her loss. It was now much more acute and absorbing. Since her visit, I heard a famous neuroscientist on the radio explain how this phenomenon can happen. When one of our sensory organs is damaged, he said, the area of the brain that had controlled that faculty cannot, as it were, tolerate its inactivity and reaches out to attach itself to a neighboring area and employs itself in a different sense perception, which thus becomes stronger. If that is so (although it has been disputed), it could account for the astonishing new skills acquired by those with impaired vision.

Our guest also declared that blind people are much more careful listeners than the sighted, because they are less distracted by appearances. They are spared the influence and pressures of facial expressions and body language, and therefore can be more independent in their judgments. In her opinion, loss of the dominant sense of sight has made her realize how many of us habitually underuse our other senses. Our eyes constantly present fresh images to us that crowd out the sensations of sound, smell, taste, and touch unless we give them full scope. Do we use to the full the senses we have?

In his delightful book *Over Hill and Dale,* the school inspector Gervase Phinn includes a remarkable poem by a blind twelve-year-old girl, who describes how her other senses help her to form visual images in her imagination. The sound of rustling leaves conjures up tall trees, splashing water evokes dolphins at play, the crackle of the fire in the grate brings to mind bright leaping flames. Smells create images of delicate blossoms, plowed earth, new-mown hay, and cows in the barn. The smell of her grandfather's pipe, her grandmother's lavender, and her mother's perfume paint precious pictures of family and home, while the flavors of food and drink bring to mind the blackness of strong coffee, the brown of toffee, the yellow of lemons, the green of melons, the red of tomatoes, the orange of carrots, and the purple of plums. Her hands feel and visualize sharp edges, smooth and slippery surfaces; cold, hard objects; warm hands, arms, and faces; the gold of the sun on her face—all of which fill her with joy as she exclaims, "I see with my ears, my nose, my mouth, my hands!"[4]

I was also told of a young man of twenty-eight who had been born with a degenerative eye disease that would lead to total blindness by the age of thirty. One day a close friend asked him what it felt like to be going blind. After a moment's thought, he made this memorable reply: "I am only losing something that I *have*; I am losing nothing of what I *am*."[5] What I am can never be taken from me; it is, in Gerard Manley Hopkins' phrase, "immortal diamond."[6] I alone can disfigure it, and God alone can transfigure and perfect its beauty.

Just as we have to listen to the promptings of the Holy Spirit and hear what the Lord God has to say to those who turn to him in their hearts, so there is an inner vision for those who seek it, and especially for the blind. In his Letter to the Ephesians, Paul prays that, "with the eyes of your heart enlightened, you may know what is the hope to which he has called you, . . . and what is the immeasurable greatness of his power for us who believe" (1:18-19).

One of the most beautiful and comforting of the visions or "shewings" described by the fourteenth-century English anchoress Julian of Norwich is of how

she saw her soul in the midst of her heart, as large as it were an endless world and a blessed kingdom and a worshipful city. In the midst of that city is our Lord Jesus, true God and true man, comely of person and

tall of stature, king and Lord of highest majesty and
honour. He sits in the soul, established in peace and
rest. And he rules and maintains heaven and earth and
all that is, without any instrument or labour. And the
soul is all occupied with the blessed Godhead which is
sovereign might, sovereign wisdom, sovereign goodness. The place that Jesus takes in our soul he shall
never remove from without end. For in us is his home-
liest home and his endless dwelling.[7]

And this must always be our inner citadel, the key of
which we give to none, silently entrusting everything to the
Lord Jesus. We may not be gifted with sights such as those
shown to Julian and many other saints, but our great need
is for an inner vision that sees beyond the confines of the
here and now; to have our minds fixed on Christ who is
above, not on the troubles here below (see Colossians 3:2).
Remember the two disciples on the road to Emmaus on
Easter Day, how they unknowingly shared a meal with the
risen Lord and recognized him at the breaking of the bread.
Then, the gospel tells us, Jesus vanished from their sight
(see Luke 24:28-31). From then on, they were to see him
with the eyes of faith. A week later, Jesus said to Thomas,
"Blessed are those who have not seen and yet have come to
believe" (John 20:29). So it is by the inner light of the Holy
Spirit that we must walk in this life, and it could be that,
like our blind houseguest, it is less outwardly distracting

for the blind than for the sighted, especially in these days of media bombardment.

We have the Lord's promise in Scripture: "I will lead the blind by a road they do not know, / by paths they have not known I will guide them. / I will turn the darkness before them into light, the rough places into level ground" (Isaiah 42:16). Because we are members of his body, Christ can use our acceptance of diminishments for the saving of others. And so, we can pray that he will use the loss of our eyesight to bring spiritual sight to those blind in spirit, and that our embracing of this disability may bring all created beings and ourselves nearer to the sight of his glory.

1. Seraphim of Sarov, quoted in Alexander (Mileant), *St. Seraphim of Sarov: Life and Teachings,* http://www .orthodoxphotos.com/readings/SOS/.

2. John Milton, "On His Blindness," http://www.bartleby .com/106/71.html.

3. William Wordsworth, "Daffodils," http://www .wordsworth.org.uk/.

4. Gervase Phinn, *Over Hill and Dale* (London: Penguin Books, Ltd, 2001).

5. Anecdote supplied by Dom Stephien Ortiger, OSB.

6. Gerard Manley Hopkins, "That Nature is a Heraclitean Fire and of the Comfort of the Resurrection," http://www .bartleby.com/122/48.html.

7. Julian of Norwich, *Revelations of Divine Love,* The Sixteenth Revelation, Chapter 67.

Chapter Four

THE SPIRITUAL SENSES

*Rejoice insofar as you are sharing Christ's
sufferings, so that you may also be glad
and shout for joy when his glory
is revealed.*

—1 Peter 4:13

Accordingto Aristotle, the primary, basic sense that belongs to all sentient beings is the sense of touch. As is true with most animals, being able to feel saves us from burning or scalding. Our sense of touch assesses temperature, alerts us to sharp objects, feels slippery or rough surfaces; it delights in playing with water, in exploring the delicacy of textures, and in embracing the beloved.

To the blind, in particular, the sense of touch is of enormous importance. It enables visually impaired people to feel and recognize objects, find their way around, and develop manual skills. It also gives other people a means of establishing contact with those who have lost their sight, communicating reassurance and love with a touch of the hand when they begin to speak to them.

All of us at times are helped by the warmth and strength of a hand clasping our own. Blessed Mother Teresa of Calcutta told the story of seeing an unhappy-looking man in the street one day. Moved by his lonely, wretched appearance, she went up to him, gently took his hand in hers, and asked, "How are you?" The man's face lit up with surprise and delight. "Oooh!" he exclaimed, "after such a long time I feel the warmth of a human hand!"[1]

Touch is a fundamental need of every human being. To be touched, hugged, and cuddled is particularly important for a baby; without it, a child's development can be tragically impaired. The reassuring touch of a mother or other primary caregiver is essential for the child to feel secure, cared for, and loved. But at every stage of our lives, we need to be affirmed and told that our lives are of value, that we are worthwhile and lovable. We may know these truths in our heads, but the experiential assurance comes through the touch of a fellow human being.

Over and over again in the gospels, we find Jesus using touch to heal the sick: laying his hands on a crippled woman (see Luke 13:11-13); anointing blind eyes with spittle (see John 9:1-7); touching lepers (see Matthew 8:1-4); taking Peter's mother-in-law by the hand and helping her up from her sickbed (see 8:14-15); putting his fingers in the ears of a deaf man and touching his tongue (see Mark 7:32-37). The blind, the deaf, and the mute were all rescued by Jesus' touch. After rising from the dead, Jesus "cures" the disciples' lack of belief by inviting them to "touch me and see; for a ghost does not have flesh and bones as you see that I have" (Luke 24:39).

The importance of touch is also illustrated by the story of the blind, deaf, and mute Helen Keller. "In the still, dark world in which I lived," she wrote, "there was no strong sentiment or tenderness. When we walk in the valley of a twofold solitude we know little of the tender affections that grow out of endearing words and actions of companionship."[2] At the age of seven, her life was transformed by Annie Sullivan, a skilled teacher who, by spelling words into her hand, gave Helen the key to every aspect of learning. At the same time, Sullivan set Helen's spirit free; at last she was able to realize that there was a whole world of knowledge and beauty outside her. An overflowing joy blossomed into Helen's first experience of love and relationship.

How important it is to know the experience of joy and delight in the beauty of the world! I remember going out one day to the hedged-in drying ground within the monastery enclosure to bring in a blanket that I had hung out to air a few days before. Underneath the grass was a thick, springy layer of moss. A lawn-proud gardener would have deplored its presence, applying chemical sprays and raking diligently to eradicate it, even though generations of flower arrangers here had been glad to collect it as a base for wreaths and other floral decorations. But apart from any usefulness, the mossy ground was a delight to walk on; the buoyant sensation under my feet gave me an irresistible impulse to dance and sing. Here was a beautiful experience of the joy we can receive from the sense of touch.

The loss or partial loss of sensation presents a real challenge to sufferers from strokes, paralysis, or neurological disorders. A trapped nerve, as in carpal tunnel syndrome, can deprive a person of sensation in the fingertips, so that he or she can't feel if a dish is too hot, can't write or sew or do so many things we take for granted. Sometimes such disabilities can be alleviated by surgery or physical therapy, sometimes not.

The Spiritual Sense of Touch

There may be no physical remedy, but there can be other modes of touch belonging to the human spirit. Theologians have spoken of spiritual senses. St. Paul told the Greeks in Athens that God had created the whole human race "so that they would search for God and perhaps grope for him and find him" (Acts 17:27). He speaks too in his letters of the eyes of our hearts (see Ephesians 1:18) and of walking in the Spirit (see Romans 8:4), while the psalmist sings, "O taste and see that the LORD is good" (Psalm 34:8). In his *Rule for Monks,* St. Benedict exhorts his disciples to bend the ear of their heart,[3] and St. Augustine frequently uses this type of language in his *Confessions.* In Book X, he writes,

> You called, shouted, broke through my deafness; you flared, blazed, banished my blindness; you lavished your fragrance, I gasped, and now I pant for you; I tasted you, and now I hunger and thirst; you touched me, and I burn for your peace.[4]

Then Augustine describes the well-known episode at Ostia when he and his mother, Monica, were talking together of God and eternal life:

> As we talked and panted for the eternal Wisdom, we just touched the edge of it by the utmost leap of our hearts; then, sighing and unsatisfied, we left the first-

fruits of our spirit captive there, and returned to the noise of articulate speech, where a word has beginning and end.[5]

The experience is one that takes Augustine out of time and the multiplicity of our present life to the unity of eternity, and "touch" is the way he describes it.

Many spiritual writers use such terminology. There is a short fourteenth-century treatise on prayer called the *Epistle of Privy Counsel* (almost certainly written by the author of the *Cloud of Unknowing*), which contains the following instruction to his disciple:

Take good, gracious God as he is, plat and plain as a plaster, and lay it to thy sick self as thou art. Or, bear up thy sick self as thou art and try for to touch by desire good, gracious God as he is, the touching of whom is endless health, by witness of the woman in the gospel: "If I touch but the hem of his clothing, I shall be safe" [Mark 5:28].[6]

How often do we ourselves speak of being "struck" or "touched" by some word or event? This may be metaphorical language, but sometimes it seems to have a mysterious dimension. You hear it described as a "touch of God." A man who had been betrayed and deserted by his wife once told me that he had reached the depths of despair, when one night, sitting alone on his bed, he distinctly felt the touch of a hand on his and the enveloping warmth and assurance of the love of Jesus. This experience transformed him totally, and its effect has remained. In the same way, people will sometimes tell you that they clearly heard a voice speaking to them that changed their lives. However you think of it, there can be no doubt that such experiences are a vehicle of God's saving grace.

Becoming the Aroma of God

Another source of joy and healing can come from our sense of smell. At its most basic level, this sense is given us as a warning of danger: danger from fire, poison, or pollution. Many animals possess it much more acutely than do humans, for it is critical for their survival. In fact, I suppose that all the senses we share with animals are less keen for us than for irrational creatures, because we have the ability to supplement them with reasoning.

I have read that the part of the brain that controls the organs of smell is the most primitive region of the brain, and I have sometimes wondered if this may be why smells and fragrances have such evocative properties. The scent of new-mown hay, for example, recalls childhood memories of traditional haymaking and the joys of playing with other children among the haystooks or riding atop a fully laden cart on its way for stacking. The smell of freshly baked bread or the aroma of cooking can stir up memories of family meals and old-time conversations around the dinner table. An elusive perfume powerfully evokes the presence of someone we once knew yet cannot now fully identify, while the tang of the sea or the smell of rain on parched earth can be almost unbearably poignant. The fragrance of wall-flowers, sweet peas, or honeysuckle or the faint and delicate scent of snowdrops and primroses can transport us to dearly loved gardens of the past and to experiences long forgotten. There is a healing in such memories, which aromatherapists know how to utilize when they incorporate the fragrant essential oils of flowers and aromatic plants in their treatments.

Although our ability to smell is sometimes less acute as we grow older, it is not so common to lose it entirely. Yet, this does happen to some people, perhaps as the result of an infection. As well as losing the warning signals that are the primary purpose of this sense, the person no longer experiences the delight of recognition or the enrichment of associations that also accompany it. Is there perhaps an inner perception we can develop to compensate for such a loss?

A woman who had lost her sense of smell suggested to me that an inner perception of the sense of smell can be discovered by reflecting on the scent of aromatic plants. In these plants, the scent is contained in the leaves rather than the flowers, but the leaves must be crushed in order to release the fragrance. The smell of plants, such as the artemisias, often contains a bittersweet element, like incense offered to God in adoration. The memory of this kind of fragrance, she said, can help those whose sense of smell is impaired to realize that the acceptance of their loss can rise like incense before God in adoration, which then becomes a sharing in the sacrifice of Christ on the cross. St. Paul says, "We are the aroma of Christ to God among those who are being saved; . . . a fragrance from life to life" (2 Corinthians 2:15-16). St. Augustine comments, "When a prayer is sincerely uttered by a faithful heart, it rises like incense from a sacred altar."[7]

And, like Mary of Bethany, who anointed the feet of Jesus with nard so that the house was filled with its fragrance (see John 12:1-3), we, too, leave the fragrance of Christ behind us when we love and serve others. Our loving care for them is "a fragrant offering and sacrifice to God" (Ephesians 5:2).

For our part, it may help to remember that the sensual experience of smells is closely linked to our breath, and the dynamics of breathing can take us to the level of our soul where prayer takes shape. Breathing rhythmically and peacefully can by degrees take us to that deep center of our being where the creating Spirit of God is forever calling us out of nothingness into life. In baptism we became, as Scripture says, temples of the Holy Spirit, who, with the Father and the Son, made his dwelling place in us (see Ephesians 2:21-22). In Christian tradition, the mystery of the Trinity is understood as God the Father speaking his Word in its entirety and thus begetting his Son in whom all the fullness of God was pleased to dwell (see Colossians 1:19). Knowing and loving each other totally, Father and Son breathe forth their own common Spirit of Love and Truth. It is through our incorporation into the incarnate Son that we enter into this eternal spiration, that we are drawn into the dance of life and love within the Godhead, and that we in turn can join in the breathing out of the Spirit on all creation. So through us, God "spreads in every place the fragrance that comes from knowing him" (2 Corinthians 2:14).

The very air we breathe is charged with the power and presence of God. As we inhale, we can be conscious of God's Spirit coming into us, filling our lungs with his divine life and power. As we exhale, we can dismiss all that is negative within us, imagining our whole body radiant and alive through breathing in God's life-giving Spirit and breathing out every kind of impurity.

The Sense of Taste and the Heavenly Banquet

Closely linked to our sense of smell is our sense of taste. It serves the same warning purpose regarding what we eat, and the same positive incentive to renew our strength with food and drink. There is also the lovely dimension of conviviality, sharing life and happiness together as we enjoy a meal with family and friends. The Bible has many references to banquets of delicious foods and fine wines, and it was not without rich implications that Jesus gave himself to his disciples in the form of bread and wine at the Last Supper.

The idea of a eucharistic meal is at the heart of the deeply thoughtful Danish film *Babette's Feast*, based on the story by Isak Dinesen. The setting is a small, remote village in the bleakness of Jutland, where for years, ancient, unrepented, and unforgiven wrongs have soured relationships within the community. A French woman has fled her wartorn home in Paris, where she has lost all she possessed, and is taken in by two maiden ladies in the village and offered a job as their cook. She is reticent about her past career, and no one knows that she had been the renowned head chef of the most fashionable restaurant in Paris. She humbly prepares meals in the unappetizing way her employers instruct her and becomes accepted by the rest of the village.

But one day, an unexpected windfall comes to her, and she asks permission to spend it on a dinner for the whole community. Never has such magnificent food and wine been seen in that village! Gradually, as the guests eat, drink, and enjoy themselves, their hardened attitudes toward one another begin to soften, and they come to realize their need for repentance and reconciliation and are able to reach out to each other in forgiveness and love. It is a foretaste of the heavenly banquet. The onetime famous chef has given all she had, and through her gesture has, in the words of one of the discerning characters in the film, "given joy to the angels," who celebrate what she has done together with the healing of those ancient quarrels.

God Hears Our Voice

Loss of voice can also be a peculiarly difficult trial, because what characterizes us as human beings is our ability to form relationships and to communicate with one another by means of speech. Our voices can embody the sharing of thoughts and feelings, and if we are unable to vocalize those thoughts and feelings, we experience a kind of imprisonment and isolation, because in a sense our voices are ourselves, and the loss of our voices cuts us off from so much that is human. We cannot express joy by singing nor grief by lamenting; we cannot speak words of comfort or encouragement to others, nor can we explain away misunderstandings or contribute creative suggestions to discussions. It is a poignant frustration, a hands-on and often searing experience of powerlessness.

Our consolation in this affliction can come, as in all our physical diminishments, from our faith in the Holy Trinity who dwells in us, in which the Father continually speaks his Word: "You are my son; today I have begotten you" (Psalm 2:7), and the Son responds: "Abba, Father!" (Mark 14:36). In the Spirit, we, too, are emboldened to whisper "Abba, Father" (see Romans 8:15) in the silence of our hearts, knowing that he has no problem in hearing us; and as St. Paul recommends, we can sing and chant to the Lord in our hearts, always and everywhere giving thanks to God our Father in the name of our Lord Jesus Christ (see Ephesians 5:19-20).

If we have lost the use of any of our senses, let us bring to mind the remembrance of past dearly loved sights, sounds, textures, smells, flavors; enjoy and embrace those memories, blessing and surrendering them to God. Remember the rhythm of things, receiving and giving back—like waves advancing and receding—just as the sense of God's presence becomes sometimes more vivid, sometimes less so. It is in the receding phase, when feeling is absent, that we grow in faith. It seems to me that people whose faculties were diminished on earth will regain them in heaven enhanced, perhaps even more than those who never lost their use. I like to tell myself that when the time comes for me to leap like a deer, I shall leap higher than all who were never disabled; I shall hear more ravishing music, see more keenly far and near, and find more delight in beauty, sight, sound, and scent and in feasting on rich, exquisitely flavored food and wine of superlative bouquet than I would ever have done if I had never known diminishment.

1. Mother Teresa of Calcutta, address given at Harvard University's Class Day Exercises, June 9, 1982, http://www.columbia.edu/cu/augustine/arch/teresa82.html.

2. Helen Keller, *The Story of My Life,* http://www.afb.org/MyLife/book.asp?ch=P1Ch4.

3. St. Benedict, *The Rule of St. Benedict,* Prologue.

4. St. Augustine, *Confessions,* trans. by Maria Boulding, (New York: New City Press, 2002), Book 10, 24.

5. St. Augustine, Book 10, 24.

6. *The Cloud of Unknowing,* Epistle of Privy Counsel and Denis Hid Divinity. ed. Dom Justin McCann, OSB (London: Orchard Books, 1924).

7. St. Augustine, Exposition on Psalm 140.

Chapter Five

THE PROCESS OF ACCEPTANCE

I am content with weaknesses, insults,
hardships, persecutions, and calamities
for the sake of Christ;
for whenever I am weak, then I am strong.

—2 Corinthians 12:10

Wisdom to cope with the diminishments and disabilities that confront us on our journey through life is not something we attain all at once. A process is necessary.

First of all, we have to do our utmost to overcome these unwelcome problems as long as possible. Accidents that leave our faculties impaired and destructive diseases that invade our bodies and diminish our personalities are painful events we should regard as obstacles to surmount rather than as trials to be accepted with resignation. We have to put up a good fight against them, taking advantage of whatever medical or surgical help is available. Some people can too easily assume that illness and disabilities are their crosses, and they must be resigned to them. They think it is unchristian and selfish to seek healing for themselves when there is so much suffering in the world. They feel that they ought to suffer and deserve to be punished for their sins.

But such thoughts are a temptation, since they exclude the remembrance that Jesus willingly took our sins and those of the whole world upon himself together with their punishment. In Julian of Norwich's vision of Christ's passion, Jesus assures her that it is to him a joy and delight that he suffered for her, and if he could suffer more he would gladly do so. Constantly meditating on those words over the following years, Julian understood that "though the

sweet manhood of Christ could suffer but once, the goodness of him can never cease to repeat the offer; every day he
is ready for the same, if it were possible."[1]

Jesus came so that we might have life to the full. We need
to be convinced that God wants us to be wholly alive and
that illness is not necessarily the cross Jesus told us to carry
after him. True enough, he said we could not be his disciples unless we took up our crosses and followed him (see
Mark 8:34). But in its original context, to carry one's cross
after Jesus meant to accept contradiction, mockery, condemnation, and death for the sake of his name. It meant to
bear with patience the opposition and ridicule encountered
by those who strive to live as faithful disciples of a crucified
master. There is indeed a bearing of the cross and following Jesus, which is the acceptance of our suffering as part
of the task of making up in our own bodies the sufferings
of Christ, for the sake of his body, the church (see Colossians 1:24). This is where the "daily" element of carrying
our cross in Luke's version of this gospel message comes in
(see Luke 9:23).

However, not everything that happens to us is the direct
will of God, and we must beware that we do not view a disease or accident that we may possibly have incurred through
our own negligence or indulgence as a punishment sent by
God. Neither should we assume that natural disasters, tragic
accidents, genetic mistakes or mutations, or the harm done
to us by human ignorance, carelessness, or malice are themselves planned by God in advance in order to punish us.

"I Will Be with You"

Of course, in the end, nothing happens without God's permissive will, and he alone knows his own mysterious purposes. If we presume to question him about unjust suffering and evil, we are likely to be given the enigmatic answer Job received that begins, "Where were you when I laid the foundation of the earth?" (Job 38:4). When we ask for reasons, God does not provide the answers. Instead, he enters into the agonizing questions with us. The one response he makes to all our interrogation is the assurance given from the beginning to the end of the Bible: "I will be with you" (Exodus 3:12; see Matthew 28:20). Our task is to have faith in this promise. In our suffering and diminishment, we become one with all our fellow sufferers in losing some quality of life. Like them, we groan to be rid of our seemingly meaningless pain but see no way that our wish can be fulfilled. Many people in this state give way to anger, bitterness, and despair; they lose sight of God and ask if this is where it will all end. Are all their struggles to no avail? If so, life is not worth living.

But if God has made himself one with us in the incarnation of his Son, then life must be worth living—how could it be otherwise? Through baptism we have been given a share in the risen life of Jesus Christ. And he, who said he would make his home in our hearts, offers his love to all who suffer. Only by believing can we transform the empty void of sickness and death into new life; this is a real sharing in the power to heal that Jesus gave to his disciples. We must believe and trust that he will be with us, according to his promise, in all the misery of our sickness, pain, and darkness.

When all is going well and the sun is shining on us, we must not be afraid to love and enjoy life fully. Nor should we feel that it is wrong to do so when the world is so full of sorrow. The Lutheran pastor Dietrich Bonhoeffer, who was executed during World War II for opposing the Nazi regime, says in a letter to a friend that we have to enjoy life's blessings to the full while they last; otherwise, we are not ready to endure loss and diminishment. Great works of literature often portray this theme: the character that has not learned to accept the joys and good things of life in simplicity and gratitude of heart can never learn to accept their loss when they are taken away.

Allowing Ourselves to Feel Our Loss

But when diminishments come, it is essential to allow ourselves time to feel them. This is comparable to the grieving stage in bereavement, which must be properly experienced, not suppressed. Therapists tell us that it is absolutely necessary to articulate our suffering. I must admit that I have always found this very difficult to do. Perhaps the British "stiff upper lip" culture and habit of understatement has something to do with it. People belonging to less reserved cultures express themselves freely by tearing their garments, shaving their beards, covering themselves with ashes, smashing crockery, howling, crying, and throwing themselves on the ground.

While we may regard such demonstration as somewhat excessive, it surely must get a lot of frustration out of their systems. But there are other, less dramatic outlets for expressing our emotions. I know a very active, busy woman who, on being diagnosed with multiple sclerosis, expressed her rage and frustration in a furious onslaught of digging and weeding in her garden with accompanying strong language. If we are fortunate, we may have a good friend who will listen with compassion without condemning our outbursts, yet encourage us to accept the situation courageously. However, indiscriminate moaning to others who have enough to bear already is no way to make the world a happier place. Writing can be another means of externalizing one's feelings without inflicting them on anyone else. Such writing, not for publication, is part of a cathartic process. Some people can pour out their feelings in music or poetry; many poets have enriched our language from their own tragic experiences, and we can sometimes borrow their words in our own situation.

We can also borrow the uninhibited language of the psalms or Job. In these books, the authors shout out what they feel to God without restraint or fear of offending the Almighty. They roundly accuse him of unfair treatment; they demand redress! Because their words are part of holy Scripture, given to us as God's word here and now, we can legitimately use them to voice our own complaints. In whatever way we react to our diminishments, we should do so honestly, not pretending to a degree of detachment we have not yet attained.

The "Passover" to Greater Life

It is only when we have exhausted all the possibilities for medical cures or healing that we can begin to tackle the next stage, which is acceptance of being diminished, disabled, ill, or helpless. Supremely difficult though it is, we must be reconciled with ourselves in this condition of sickness, disability, and aging and see ourselves as valuable and responsible, even when we are in a state of dependence on others. Our task, then, is the passage to greater life, whether through renewed health or death.

Acceptance can be a tough hurdle. Deep down, we know it is the only way forward, but it takes the grace of God and all our spiritual strength to follow that path. When we reach the point where we need to accept our circumstances, we frequently find a curious barricade confronting us. It is as if the forces of evil bar the way; there is a strange resistance to the promptings of grace, a temptation to seek diversion, to retreat into the past, like the Israelites looking back longingly to the fleshpots of Egypt and lamenting the lack of "the cucumbers, the melons, the leeks, the onions, and the garlic" (see Exodus 16:3, Numbers 11:5). Real courage is asked of us.

But we know that countless others have surmounted this hurdle, including many ordinary human beings with no greater heroism and very likely greater hardships than ours. With "so great a cloud of witnesses" to encourage us (see Hebrews 12:1), we too shall overcome. We shall find the strength to let go of plans, projects, work, ambitions, laying them down at the foot of the cross. This, too, needs to be done deliberately and quietly. In letting them go, we don't have to persuade ourselves that some of them were not good plans and projects or not worth the pangs of our unfulfilled dreams. At least they deserve a farewell blessing and thanks for the ways in which they enriched our lives. But now it is time to turn our minds to the new task God is offering us. It is a passover experience, a passage from the alienation of illness and suffering to a new and transforming relationship with God, ourselves, and others.

This is the crisis point in our suffering, a moment of supreme importance. Imagine the angels and saints in heaven waiting with bated breath, the whole of creation eagerly longing for the children of God to be revealed (see Romans 8:19), as they wait to see whether we decide to take the step that leads us forward to the realization of its meaning or backward into bitterness and despair. Our decision is the key that unlocks the meaning of our diminishments. It is a moment of great faith and trust, but it seems that the actual moment of acceptance is mysterious. We are acutely aware of it both before and after, but the act itself is hidden, indescribable. We only know that it *has* been accomplished, and by the grace of God.

From the moment we accept the diminishment, we set our faces forward, not backward. Assuredly, there is always the need to guard and reinforce our decision, since we are still free, and turning back is still a possibility. But the future opens out ahead of us with untold possibilities. And only when we have attained this acceptance will we be able to enter into the new role that God in his providence is offering us. Not only does God allow us to suffer these things, but he also offers them to us as our task, and by their acceptance we can find a meaning for them all. That meaning is unique for each person; each one of us has to discover the meaning of his or her own diminishment and agony. It can then become a blessing for others.

1. Julian of Norwich, *Revelations of Divine Love,* The Ninth Revelation, Chapter 22, http://www.ccel.org/ccel/julian/revelations.x.i.html.

Chapter Six

BECOMING A PRESENCE OF PEACE

Neither death, nor life, . . . nor height, nor depth, nor anything else in all creation, will be able to separate us from the love of God in Christ Jesus our Lord.

—Romans 8:38-39

Our senses are far from being the only faculties that can be impaired. There can also be a diminishment of vitality—of physical and mental powers—especially as we grow older. Illnesses, too many to enumerate, threaten to disrupt our lives, each leaving its own legacy of weakness and pain. I won't attempt to consider all the diseases and dysfunctions that can lie in ambush for us on our path through life. Suffice it to say that there must be a way to come to terms with them, even to make friends with them and find meaning in them all. To spread peace and joy is now our calling, and it is a task of immense value to those around us.

Illness is not, of course, the proper state of human beings. God intended us to have life to the full, to enjoy life, not poor health. We have to do everything we can to recover. But these diminishments can teach us a great deal about ourselves, revealing how much we want to live our lives on our own terms. They tell that us we are not omnipotent, that we do not always have the power to control our lives and circumstances. We are human and are often victims of life's stresses and strains. Pain is a reminder of our mortality, of our decreasing ability to do the things we had planned and the creative work we might have contributed to the pool of human achievements, had we retained our strength. And if there is no likelihood of recovery, we think of all the unfinished jobs we will have to leave for others to do, the uncompleted projects and unaccomplished plans that were so dear to our hearts.

Perhaps this is God's way of changing our sights. Instead of seeing everything in the light of this life only, we are challenged to see things in the light of our eternal destiny. For, as St. Paul says, if our hope is limited to this world only, we should be of all people the most to be pitied (see 1 Corinthians 15:19). No, the things of this world will pass away, and we must set our hearts on true joys.

I remember one of the nuns in our community who was dying of liver cancer. Though racked by the disease, she had no time for complaints or regrets; she characteristically tackled the business of dying with all her energy. Propped up where she could see it was a picture of the Eucharist with the words *Hoc Est Corpus Meum,* "This is my body." These words she repeated constantly as she offered her own ravaged body to God as her share in Christ's redeeming work. Throughout her life she had put all her passion and energy into everything she did. Now one task remained: to offer herself, body and soul, in her sickness, for Christ to suffer in her and so extend his passion into the present day. She understood that although during his earthly life, Jesus was able to live only his own limited human experience, in the Eucharist he has become one with each of us and shares every detail and facet of our existence, including our diminishments, illnesses, and old age. This he could not do in his mortal flesh, but by coming to dwell in our inmost being, he has prolonged his own humanity by placing himself in our contemporary situation.

Learning to Be Gentle with Ourselves

When we are ill, we must be gentle with ourselves. This is not the time for bodily mortifications and penances. Our bodies are our faithful partners and must be nursed to health. Our minds, too, sometimes need relaxing. I once knew a sick priest who would put aside his serious reading in the afternoon and invite the Lord to read a "whodunit" with him. This is not to say we may permit ourselves unbridled self-indulgence. We still have to transcend ourselves, to die to self-love even when we are ill. But this is more likely to be through refraining from complaining, from making unreasonable demands on those around us, from being fractious and impossible to please, and from criticizing.

In some ways, disability and illness are easier to cope with when you are completely out of action and need to be looked after by others. The difficult time is when you are approaching that stage, when you must struggle to keep going, to carry out your normal duties, and to take part in your usual routines. You may be expending tremendous effort, but you may feel, rightly or wrongly, that it is scarcely noticed or appreciated by those around you. Then, if you allow yourself a little respite, you wonder whether you are giving in to weakness and should try to be more heroic, or whether you should simply ask to be relieved of your duties. How hard it is to be completely simple!

We may have to accept that we are unable to do our share in the work of the house. However, we always have the opportunity to show love and consideration to others. We can do this by graciously accepting their help and bearing our condition with sweetness and peace, so that they who are perhaps overstressed and burdened may feel their load is lightened instead of increased.

Becoming a presence of peace and sweetness is not automatic; we can remain imprisoned in self-pity and resentment. Then there are those days when we seem to get out of bed on the wrong side and feel impatient and fed up with everything. All our good desires and endeavors have flown out of the window. We seem to be plodding through a dreary vale of misery, feeling very alone. It is a time of waiting for deliverance, a time of trusting that the Holy Spirit will come down once more and renew us and that—in that lovely image of St. Hildegard of Bingen—he will make our spirits green again, sending out shoots and flowers ready for the fruit to come. Perhaps we need to be kinder to ourselves, not blaming ourselves for our failures, resting not only our bodies but also our spirits. Meanwhile we can, in our hearts, bless our neighbors, those we encounter, those who serve us, and those who don't think of it.

So, let us not think about diseases and disasters, wars and hostility, but fill our minds with thoughts of peace and beauty, visualizing the life of the risen Christ coursing through our veins and overflowing to the world. To spread peace and joy is now our calling, and it is a task of immense value to our neighbors. We are called to be always the same—serene, smiling, and uncomplaining, never gossiping, judging, or condemning, but always having a good word for others, taking the time to listen to other people, and realizing that they, too, have needs and desires. Then we shall be a tower of strength, a light in the encroaching darkness to those around us, surrounding them with an atmosphere in which they can work to bring about the kingdom of God.

Bearing Witness to Divine Life through Intercession

We may be physically weak, unable to concentrate for long, falling asleep over our prayers, forgetting things, but we still have a spiritual job to do: first, to bear witness to the divine life within us by accepting our condition in patience and graciousness; then, to intercede for others. How many needs there are in the world and all about us, how much there is to intercede for! People turn to us instinctively in their distress; the many requests posted daily on our Web site and bulletin board are evidence of their faith in our prayers. The church looks to the sick and elderly to pray for God's blessing on its preaching, teaching, healing, and reconciling ministries. Sometimes we receive impassioned pleas to storm heaven, remaining as it were on our knees day and night praying innumerable rosaries and making endless novenas for particular intentions.

In our frail, diminished condition we could be overwhelmed if we thought that God had to be continually reminded of all these needs. If we tried to hold each one before his face with the strength of our uninterrupted concentration, we would soon be burnt out and unable to pray at all. But that is not what intercession means. It means entering into the prayer of Jesus, who is interceding for us at the right hand of God (see Romans 8:34; Hebrews 8:1, 9:24). Our petitions are subsumed into his. Our part is to hand over all these intentions and requests so that they are incorporated into his own. We have to seat ourselves with him at the Father's right hand, and unite our intentions for all those we wish to pray for with his own prayer. There is no need to reiterate names and case histories; God knows about them already. Rather, we must concentrate on being united with Jesus, trusting that in his goodness and love he will not forget any of them.

At times, one particular intention may be uppermost in our minds and insist on our attention. Then we can place it in Jesus' hands, confident that he hears and wants to give far more than we can ask or deserve. To be tense and agitated, afraid of forgetting someone who has asked our prayers, is really an indication that we attach too much importance to our own efforts. We can be quite sure that although our memory may let us down, God's will not. All we need to do is renew our intentions daily with what St. Thérèse of Lisieux described as "a surge of the heart,"[1] asking God to reveal his loving kindness to all he has put into our hearts, all who have asked and rely on our prayers, and all who are in any kind of need. As we keep our attention on the Father, we pray with the risen Christ for the coming of his kingdom and the fulfillment of his will, on earth as in heaven.

When Cardinal Joseph Bernardin lay terminally ill of pancreatic cancer in a Chicago hospital, he sent out an urgent message to the people of his archdiocese and to all the friends he had made through his ministry. "Pray urgently for the sick and the dying," he told them, "because they are unable to pray for themselves. They are utterly overwhelmed by pain, distress, and fear of what is to come."[2] Pray, that is, not so much *for* the sick and dying as *in their name and in their stead*, for we are members of one another and every prayer we make is made for each member of the body as well as for ourselves.

As he hung on the cross, Christ suffered, prayed, and offered himself to his Father in the name of all whom the Father had given him—every man, woman, and child he had redeemed and incorporated into himself. Consequently, each of us can pray in the name of Jesus our Head, and in this prayer, too, the sick and the dying today are included. St. Augustine never tired of teaching his people about the "whole Christ," who cries out to God from the ends of the earth (see Psalm 61:2), not only in pain and distress but also in praise and thanksgiving.

By reading the Old Testament, we know that the Hebrews recognized that God had redeemed them and formed them into a people he could call his own. They were not only the people of Israel, they were the corporate personality of Israel itself. And so, Augustine tells us, in the psalms we find the voice of a single man lamenting, complaining, praying, longing, praising and thanking God, and expecting his help. Jesus in his human nature embodies these prayers of the psalms and prays them in the name of us all. For those we know and the many we do not know personally, we can pray in many ways, and above all in the prayer of the church, the Divine Office, applying the words of the psalms to ourselves and to all humankind who form one body in Christ.

When we are elderly and sick, we are called more than ever to walk in the Spirit, to listen constantly to the promptings of the Holy Spirit in our hearts inviting and urging us to transcend our own weakness and inclination to give up and settle for self-pity, asking us to love our neighbor in whatever way his grace inspires us. However feeble or senile we may be, we are still God's children, and there is that in us that is yet "immortal diamond."[3]

The British theologian Donald Nicholl tells of a man, gravely ill in the hospital, whom the doctors were treating with various new drugs in the hope of a cure. The drugs had such a terrifying effect on the man that he thought he was going to lose his mind. All that seemed to remain of his former self was but a tiny particle, surrounded by total darkness and chaos. As he lay in his bed, desperately hanging on to his sanity, he suddenly heard a voice in the nearby corridor moaning, "I'm so bloody lonely I could cry." An old miner, hospitalized for the first time in his life, had been left in a wheelchair, awaiting attention. The impersonality of the whole system had overwhelmed him. From the deep pit of his own terror, the desperately sick man in the ward said to himself, "I'll go and sit with him if it's the last thing I do." He got out of bed and went into the corridor to bring what he could of empathy and comradeship to the old man. From that moment, his own fears began to abate. In the voice of the miner, he had heard the voice of God calling him to wholeness through a caring relationship with a fellow sufferer.[4]

Choosing Gratitude, Light, Life

It is easy to slip into a negative, complaining frame of mind when we are ill or our plans are frustrated. Every day we need to make a deliberate choice to accept all that happens to us—especially the things that irritate and test us beyond all bearing—to choose them over and over again, to renew our commitments, to accept and thank God for all he sends us. Once we get into the habit of thanking God for everything, we gain strength and vitality for our souls and discover that nothing can separate us from the love of Christ (see Romans 8:38-39). How important it is constantly to choose everything that happens rather than merely enduring it, grousing about it, or being resigned to it! Our life consists of continual choices. It is up to us to ensure that we choose light and not darkness, life and not death.

Our choices must be for the spreading of God's kingdom and for the building up of his church rather than for pulling down not only ourselves but those who need the encouragement of our witness. It is up to us to choose to be positive in the face of mediocrity and cynicism, not settling for the least effort. Poor health can make this choosing a real challenge, even to the point of heroism, but we must not make the mistake of thinking that it makes no difference in the big picture. The angels and saints have the vantage point of heaven, of seeing in advance the working out of God's plan through the lives of the poor and needy, those whom Scripture calls the *anawim*—the nameless humble people who are waiting with longing for the Lord's coming. The sick can make up for the materialism and unmindfulness of so many by the intensity of their longing for the Spirit of Life, the Spirit that transforms all weakness and burns away all dross. Their only pressing tasks throughout their lives are to acknowledge the sovereign rule of the omnipotent God, and to advance God's kingdom by giving him absolute mastery over them. So, let us try to redeem the time, as St. Paul says (see Ephesians 5:16), transforming each moment with an act of love.

St. Teresa of Ávila constantly stressed the need to make a strong resolution to love and serve God and neighbor no matter how one felt. St. Thérèse of Lisieux demonstrated this teaching daily, believing that nothing was too small to be lived out of love and offered to God.

When I was in the novitiate, a holy old monk never tired of telling us that we can't do very much, but we must do what we can. Even if we are alone in our efforts, our contribution to the coming of the kingdom is indispensable. Each of us may be only one small person, but we *are* one, and each one counts. Some people make the world a better place simply by being in it.

1. Thérèse of Lisieux, quoted in *Catechism of the Catholic Church*, 2558.

2. Cardinal Joseph Bernardin, *Journey to Peace* (New York: Doubleday, 1996).

3. Gerard Manley Hopkins, "That Nature is a Heraclitean Fire and of the Comfort of the Resurrection," http://www.bartleby.com/122/48.html.

4. Donald Nicholl, *Holiness* (London: Darton, Longman & Todd, 1981).

Chapter Seven

GOD HAS NOT FINISHED WITH US YET

*Even though our outer nature is wasting away,
our inner nature is being renewed
day by day.*

—2 Corinthians 4:16

People say you are not old until you are in your nineties; in fact, the time is not far off when you will have to be a centenarian before you are reckoned to be an old person. Being old, however, surely depends on your attitude as well as your health.

I have known old people who are interested in everything; they are open to new ideas, ready to meet new people and share their concerns. They keep up their hobbies, enjoy exchanging reminiscences, laughing over the things they did when they were young. These are people who have grown in wisdom and maturity with the years and are at peace with themselves. They have accepted their lives with all the choices they made or their parents made for them, including those that may have proved to be mistaken—together with all their consequences—and accepted them without regrets, resentments, or giving way to the "if only" syndrome. Grateful for all the good in their lives, they have found freedom of spirit, and it shows in their faces.

On the other hand, most of us have met old people who have failed the test. They complain about everything, dwell on ancient grievances, refuse to forgive, and are deeply embittered. They tyrannize with guilt those family members who attempt to live their own lives and seek their own fulfillment. To see these unhappy people or attempt to talk to them is to realize how easily we can be engulfed by negativity unless we have constantly practiced acceptance—choosing to forgive and let go.

We can't wait until we are ninety to learn that this is the key to wisdom and contentment. Those who have found the key have not only found peace themselves but have become a haven for others, especially the young, who instinctively confide in them in the assurance that they will not meet with indifference, incomprehension, or disapproval. Young people know that their old, wise friend is young at heart, ready to encourage them and help them discern the way forward.

Learning to Accept Our Circumstances

Many old people, of course, find themselves alone, having outlived their families and contemporaries, and they are often without any significant contacts. It is important for them to realize that they are not, in fact, isolated. They are living cells of the body of Christ, and, as such, have an intrinsic value whether or not they have any material interaction with others. As St. Paul tells us, the life and death of each of us has its influence on others (see Romans 14:7). The spiritual vigor of each cell contributes to the vitality of the whole body; the converse is also soberingly true.

To know how to grow old is surely the master work of wisdom, but it is one of the most difficult of arts. We must accept our years instead of wanting to be thought younger than we are. We have all met elderly people who attempt to deceive themselves and others by dressing in a way that may have been appropriate at one time but now only causes ridicule or pity. The reason for this is surely the premium set on youth by our culture. With its emphasis on achievement and production, contemporary Western culture has little esteem or respect for old age, whereas Eastern values are much more centered on wisdom and contemplation. In the East, old people have traditionally been held in great reverence. In some African tribal cultures, grandparents also enjoy an honorable status as they take over the education of the children of the community, leaving the mothers free to work the land and harvest the crops and the fathers to hunt for food. In these cultures, seniors are respected for their long experience of life. They form, as it were, the collective memory of the tribe, a link between generations. Thus they make an important contribution to community decisions, and their old age is happy in the security of knowing that they have their place and their value.

Until the twentieth century, grandparents living in Western cultures normally continued to live in their own homes and to be cared for by their children. Difficult and cantankerous though they may sometimes have been, they had their own assured place in the family. Today both parents often have professional careers or are obliged to work in order to provide for their children and pay the mortgage. It is increasingly common for the old folks to live in assisted living centers or nursing homes, where they can receive the professional care their families cannot provide. It is not that children don't want their parents at home, but that they are often unable to give them the care that they need. Usually, old people are extremely reluctant to "go into a home." Leaving their familiar surroundings and routine can be a severe trauma, and they may have difficulty coping with such a change. They feel set aside, unwanted, and no longer of any value to society. They can suffer from internal emptiness, anxiety, and pain. Lacking strength, energy, or interest in reading or other activities may spawn feelings of worthlessness, depression, or rebellion, which may also overwhelm them.

Most of us have seen the T-shirt with the slogan proclaiming, "Old Age Is Not for Sissies." As we age, we are stripped more and more of the things we clung to: our work, talents, ministry, career, authority, gifts, influence. Who would voluntarily renounce any of these? Such stripping should, of course, make it progressively easier to leave this mortal life. The more luggage we lose, the lighter we travel to God. However, we still have to live our lives while they last.

Age can indeed be an even greater spiritual challenge than youth. Everything is harder, more demanding of patience and graciousness, without the strength to fall back on or the power to recover the energy we expend. We find ourselves unable to remember names or where we have put things, even what day of the week it is, so that we begin to wonder if we are in the early stages of dementia or Alzheimer's disease. We are embarrassed by undignified ailments. We find ourselves obliged to accept help from others, a humiliation for those of us who value our independence.

Chapter 7

The Grace of Dependence

I remember being in a hospital years ago, recovering from major surgery, when I experienced what it means to be totally dependent on others. Too weak to do the most basic things for myself, I needed the assistance of nurses and attendants. I also counted on the members of my community to bring me clean clothes, books, and whatever else I needed and to keep me in touch with what was going on at home. This experience was a real grace, revealing not only the kindness of other people but also the knowledge of my own neediness.

Normally, we can cope reasonably well with our daily routine and chores, and we do not like to have others doing things for us. Certainly we have no right to expect others to wait on us without necessity, but a reminder of that primeval rebellion of human beings against submitting to God's ordinances is a salutary thing, and I was grateful for it. "Isn't she wonderful?" people may say of the disabled who succeed in achieving a measure of independence, and it is indeed a great satisfaction for the disabled to do things for themselves. But to be dependent and helpless is also a grace. It is important for us to see ourselves as valuable and responsible even when we are in a state of dependence on others. Most of the time, we never manage to let go of control. We cling to our own strength and capabilities; even when we pray, we are still trying to fix things. But when we realize that we are, in fact, not in control and have little power to do anything anymore, then we recognize that God is in charge and that he alone is our strength. His presence will not necessarily fix things or eliminate the need for human assistance, but it assures us that all will be well.

During our active years, we often longed for an opportunity to be still and receptive, but pressures of work constantly compelled us to be oriented toward "getting things done." Now that we are old and no longer able to get much of anything done, our contribution to the life of our family and those with whom we live must be on a different level. All the relinquishments of old age are renunciations of action, not of heart and mind. They are renunciations of doing, not of being. When we think of the things we used to do, the tasks entrusted to us, our achievements and accomplishments, how others relied on us for help and support, we can feel altogether useless, and a burden on our families and communities. We must not allow ourselves to think these thoughts; it is a temptation that we have to resist with all our strength.

No matter how diminished we are, our essential value remains the same: we are created by God as his beloved children, and nothing can ever take this dignity from us. What is more, God has not finished with us yet! Instead of these dispirited thoughts, it is surely better to thank God for all that was good in our lives and ask forgiveness for the sins and failures that disfigured it, trusting in his love to supply what was lacking as well as the good we failed to do. It is true that many of our undertakings remain unfinished, and we realize that we will never be able to complete them. This feeling of being unfulfilled can be so painful, harder to accept than old age itself. But this, too, we must choose courageously, otherwise we shall block our growth. Life moves only forward. Every stage of life has to be lived as fully and resolutely as possible, including old age. Only then shall we be ready to be "gathered to our fathers, having lived our full span of years" (see Genesis 25:8, 35:29).

The Importance of Revisiting the Past

If we are honest with ourselves, we will acknowledge that we have failed to live each stage of our lives as fully and generously as we could. There is a good deal of unfinished business in our past; not only the plans and projects, the creative work of hands and mind that we had hoped to leave to posterity, but also the state of our relationships with others and with God. There was never enough time, and we were always too busy.

One of the most important tasks of the autumn of our lives is to revisit the past, taking the time and opportunity to reminisce, traveling back in memory to our earliest years and each subsequent period. At each stage, we have to try to recall what was good and beautiful there, in nature, in our families, and in other people, not forgetting the good things we ourselves may have done with the help of God's grace. We must stay peacefully with each memory of happiness and love, thanking God for these precious gifts, then ask his forgiveness for past sins of ingratitude, neglect and unkindness, pride, self-deception, or lack of love.

We also have to remember what was painful in those years, things we can hardly bear to recall—pain that others have caused us or, worse still, that we have caused them. With our hand in God's, we need to confront these memories bravely and honestly without trying to avoid or gloss over anything, bringing all of them fully to Christ and laying them down at his feet, whether it is a matter of our own sins, the sins of other people, or those cruelly timed, senseless misfortunes that go by the name of Murphy's Law.

There is still much to be forgiven in our past. Now in our old age, if we have not done so before, God is asking us to accept and forgive all, handing everything over to him, thanking and praising him even for these memories, because he was there and suffered them with us. We need to take plenty of time over this all-important task; to search out things that are hiding in corners, to be completely honest, banishing all excuses and pretenses.

It can be helpful to write down these memories as we work our way through them, not with any thought of publishing our memoirs, which would probably not be of any great interest, but simply to externalize them. By doing so, we can achieve a certain distance from them. Then we should deliberately burn what we have written, making a burnt offering to the Lord of our painful memories. We have recalled and dealt with them—forgiven the hurts we sustained, accepted and repented of the guilt of our own past actions, prayed for God's healing and blessing on all involved, including ourselves, and thanked God for his grace poured out. At the end of this process of gathering up and healing our memories and regrets, we will find ourselves liberated from past pain, set free to welcome and listen to others without fear and without judgment and to travel with them on their own journey to peace.

We are all fellow sufferers, each bearing our wounds and scars and remaining vulnerable to the recurring assaults of the demons of the past. But we know that they have no further power over us as long as we grant them no admittance. This is a matter of faith, not feelings; it has to be renewed and held firmly whenever the old temptations to anger, resentment, and refusal threaten to invade us again. We must each claim our intrinsic value as a child of God, saying to ourselves, These demons are threatening me again, but they cannot overcome me because the Lord is my rock and my refuge; he made me, he died for me, his body was broken and his blood poured out for me; therefore, nothing can separate me from him. These feelings are simply my *old unregenerate self*. But God has poured his own Spirit into my heart, and I have decided to live by the Spirit, which is the life of Jesus within me, even if I feel churned up and all but overwhelmed. I am determined to stand firm.

We are able now to live in the present, to celebrate the work of God's grace in our lives, to turn from the successes and failures of former times to the promises of Christ, filling our minds and hearts with thoughts of the day when God will wipe away every tear from our eyes, when death will be no more, when there will be neither mourning nor crying nor pain, for the former things will have passed away (see Revelation 21:4).

Our Work Has Not Ended

We must see old age as something God has called us to and trust in his grace, which is always available. It is not a matter of enduring passively, waiting for death. We are called to utilize the energy that is left and refuse to accept a diminishment of our being. As long as we live, we shall still be subject to trials, temptations, little deaths. When we are old and infirm, we are more than ever called to build up the kingdom of God. There are still many opportunities for us to contribute to God's creative work. Each of us can work toward making our world more human. If we are no longer able to *do* things, we can concentrate on *relating* to other people, listening attentively to them, and taking an interest in them, making them feel appreciated and valued, finding joy in giving encouragement. Not only do people have a deep need for such relationships, but our own lives are immeasurably enriched and liberated by them.

I often think of a story told by Jean Vanier, the founder of the L'Arche communities, about his friend who had just completed a doctorate in philosophy and was looking forward to a brilliant and prestigious teaching career when he was diagnosed with a brain tumor. A delicate operation removed the tumor but left him unable to read. For two years, he was plunged into confusion, rage, and rebellion. His whole life was ruined, and he was completely disoriented. But little by little he began to discover that happiness and fulfillment can also be found in relating to others and entering into their joys and sorrows, hopes and fears. The time finally came when he could say to his friend, "Now I can accept what has happened. In the past I used to live for intellectual pursuits and ideas; now that I am no longer able to read, I live with and for other people, and I am content and even happy."[1] His life became one of listening to people in difficulties and supporting them. He had come to terms with the loss of his academic career.

In the evening of their lives, the old are called to the greatest task of all, namely to bear witness in the midst of their weakness and suffering to the presence of the Holy Spirit in their hearts, and so to spread God's kingdom on earth. The past is in God's merciful hands, and they no longer need to worry about it. Their eyes are now focused on the future. Through their joyous faith in God's promises and their compassion for those who bear the heavy burdens of the day, they are like a lamp in a dark place, a beacon of encouragement to others.

When my mother was old and living alone, her parish priest told her how much he counted on the prayers of his senior parishioners, who, he said, were like Aaron and Hur holding up the arms of Moses as he took his stand on the hilltop, interceding for the Israelites fighting on the plain below. As long as Moses kept his arms raised, Israel had the advantage; but when he let his arms droop, the Amalekites prevailed. So when Moses grew weary, Aaron and Hur supported his arms on either side so that they remained unwavering till Joshua and his army defeated Amalek (see Exodus 17:8-13). My mother, who was a woman of great faith, took this example to heart; her task in old age would be to sustain the priests in the front line of the spiritual battle.

It is also the role of the old and the sick, in particular, to be the embodiment and symbol of the church, faithfully keeping watch for the return of her Lord, when Christ will come again to gather his people to himself and lead them to heaven, where all will be made new. It was the conscious expectation of the first Christians that Christ would come again in their lifetime, and in those days their united prayer was "Maranatha! Come, Lord Jesus!"

After two thousand years, perhaps our expectation has grown dim, and it is our task in old age to keep it brightly glowing, making that prayer our own so that it becomes the voice of the faithful Bride waiting and longing for her Beloved to return. Scripture even urges us to hasten Christ's second coming. "Since all these things are to be dissolved in this way, what sort of persons ought you to be in leading lives of holiness and godliness, waiting for and hastening the coming of the day of God? . . . But, in accordance with his promise, we wait for new heavens and a new earth, where righteousness is at home" (2 Peter 3:11-13).

In midlife we have so many duties and responsibilities that the idea of hastening the end of the world is scarcely one of our priorities. But in old age our task becomes simpler (though not less challenging). What we are called to do now is to try to increase the amount of love in the world. Blessed Mother Teresa of Calcutta never tired of saying that it is not how much we do, but how much love we put into our actions that will accomplish this task. Where there is no compassion, no care for the suffering of others, our endeavor must be to put compassion and love.

Perhaps we should also ask ourselves why some people seem to be so unkind and callous toward others. Rather than passing self-righteous judgment on them, we might try asking ourselves what terrible wounds such people must have suffered in their own lives, especially their childhood, that have caused them to behave in such a way. Only God knows and understands. We need to pray earnestly that he will change their hearts and put a little kindness there and, at the same time, put understanding and pity in our own.

But are we always ready to hear his response? "Come," he says to us now, "I am sending *you* to show my healing love to all who suffer—oppressor and victim alike." We have received mercy and kindness from God; now he commissions us to show kindness and mercy in our turn to others—a task we can only fulfill through his power at work in us. We must have faith in our mission and in the power of God.

As our earthly lives draw to an end, we ourselves are called to be a sign that the kingdom of God is already here, a witness to the peace Christ won by his victory over sin and death, which he freely shared with those who trust in his word. We may not have any direct influence on world events, but a quiet heart that is rooted in this peace is an irresistible attraction to others in our strife-torn world and can bring new hope to many.

1. Jean Vanier, *Toute Personne est une Histoire Sacrée* (Paris: Plon, 1994).

Chapter Eight

DISCOVERING OUR ROLE

*I endure everything for the sake of the elect,
so that they may also obtain the salvation that is
in Christ Jesus, with eternal glory.*

—2 Timothy 2:10

If we question God with our repeated, Why does he allow all the suffering, the injustice, the evil in our world? we have to be prepared for his response. He will call upon us to be the agents of his deliverance, perhaps by learning to have the compassion that opens our eyes to see what part we can play and to be unstinting in our effort to help those who are suffering.

We often see compassion stirred up when disaster strikes. In these days of instant global communication, we are becoming much more aware of catastrophic events, which often seem to arouse unrecognized powers in people that enable them to transcend danger in order to rescue others. While the world reels with shock at the news of earthquakes, floods, fires, and famines, hundreds of nameless volunteers are already on their way to help in the rescue work. Often these are ordinary people, who make extraordinary efforts to save lives and discover qualities of caring and compassion in themselves that had previously seemed dormant or nonexistent.

It was heartwarming to see the generosity of the world-wide response to the Indian Ocean tsunami of December 26, 2004. For a time, almost everyone on earth seemed to be united in the effort to give help and care to the stricken. We heard or read stories of amazing heroism in people wounded themselves, who spontaneously risked their own lives to save others. Similar stories were told about the aftermath of the events on September 11, 2001. On that day, many experienced a personal transformation that gave them the incentive and the will to transcend their own trauma and reach out to others in need. The terrorist attack acted like a catalyst, reinvigorating people and helping them find new strength to help others. The media recorded for us the marvels of the selfless efforts of many people to rescue victims and care for the injured and bereaved.

On a smaller scale, I heard not too long ago of a homeless teenager who intercepted the knife of a drunken man who was aiming it at a young woman on a crowded street. The teenager's action seemed almost instinctive, yet it brought to light a courage and a generosity no one would have thought possible in someone who had been essentially rejected by society. It cost the boy his life, but he surely received a hero's welcome in the land of the living.

There are other stories of hidden goodness shown by people in prisons, on the streets, or indeed in ordinary walks of life, where the potential for unselfish caring is not always apparent. I once witnessed an act of kindness that appeared to be more of a deliberate choice than an instinct. Waiting on a train station platform where another train was filling up with passengers, ready to depart, I saw a tall, well-dressed man carrying a briefcase, running at top speed to board his train. At the same moment, a young delivery boy appeared with a large tray laden with produce. The two collided, and the contents of the tray rolled far and wide.

Inner conflict was plain to see on the main's face; evidently it was imperative for him to catch this train, yet here was this youngster struggling not to cry, facing the prospect of not just the loss of the goods entrusted to him, but also the probability of having his wages docked, or even of losing his job. I watched in fascination, but it was no more than a second before the man turned back, began chasing the scattered items, and restored them to the tray. With an encouraging smile at the boy, he pressed his shoulder briefly and rushed after his train. (I couldn't see if he caught it, but fervently hoped that the angels delayed it for him.)

Oftentimes, disasters only increase the selfishness of those who are out to exploit them by looting and pillaging. But human beings are not so simply put into categories of "good" and "bad," as some old-fashioned novelists portray them. Stories of heroic sanctity came from the death camps of Nazi Germany and Soviet Russia, and some who think nothing of stealing and robbing will help others who are down and out and show great gentleness to the weak. There are people who are neither better nor worse than their neighbors in daily life, who will expend all their strength, refusing to give up until they have saved every victim of a climbing accident, hurricane, fire, or mining disaster.

Finding God's Purpose for Our Lives

We may lack the physical strength or the opportunity to take part in rescue operations like these, but surely real heroism is shown by the injured and wounded who endure perhaps a lifetime of pain and helplessness without self-pity, in quiet trust that God will accept it as their share in the sufferings of Christ for the world's redemption. Each person can do some good that no one else can do. Cardinal Joseph Bernardin once wrote urgently to his people,

> My dear brothers and sisters, who will bring light to dispel the darkness of our world? If not you and me, then who? And if not now, today, then when? We are the instruments God uses to dispel the world's darkness. There are no others. So even if what we do might seem insignificant, our effort is needed. Let us, then, live up to our responsibilities.[1]

We each have a role in God's overall purpose, and whatever happens to us or is taken from us is incorporated into that role. God never seems to let us know in advance what this is or how it will all turn out. He requires us to take a step of faith at every crisis in our life. If you think of the great biblical characters such as Abraham, Isaac, and Jacob, you can see they were people whose lives were not free of mistakes and blemishes, but they believed in God's promises. So with us: using our own unique gifts and place in history we can touch people and do good in a way that no one else can do. We can each become a light-bearer to those near us.

In a famous passage, John Henry Newman wrote,

God has created me to do him some definite service. He has committed some work to me which he has not committed to another. I have my mission. I may not know it in this life, but I shall be told it in the next. He has not created me for naught. Whatever, wherever I am, I can never be thrown away. If I am in sickness, my sickness may serve him; in perplexity, my perplexity may serve him. He does nothing in vain. He knows what he is about.[2]

I think we can all identify with what Cardinal Newman is saying. We each have our task, our role, our mission in life. This is not something spelled out to us beforehand; we have to discover it. It seems as if affliction and suffering can serve to open our eyes to realities to which we had formerly been blind. Perhaps our lives had been geared to the attainment of success or status. We might have wanted to advance our careers and projects to make a unique contribution to science, literature, or the arts. We might have merely desired to safeguard our assets and enjoy the good things the world offered. But now, perhaps, God could be using our suffering to lift us up to a different plane of understanding and direct our eyes to a greater vision.

When conflicts and disasters occur, people are apt to demand that God should intervene like a *deus ex machina* and put all to rights. How often have we heard people ask: "Why doesn't God stop the terrorists, divert the suicide bombers, strike down the oppressors or the human traffickers and drug dealers?" And yet, if we read the Bible carefully, we can find many stories of God's deliverance being dependent on human cooperation.

In the most famous of these stories, the account of the Exodus, the Hebrews are crushed under the burden of forced labor and harsh taskmasters, and we hear them crying out to God from their slavery. God was by no means deaf to their prayers; he had seen their affliction and was determined to deliver them. But instead of coming down from heaven himself and striking the Egyptians dead, he commissioned Moses to confront Pharaoh and order him to let God's people go a three days' journey into the desert to offer sacrifice to God. Like anyone else given such a mission, Moses protested vigorously: "Who am I that I should go to Pharaoh, and bring the Israelites out of Egypt?" (Exodus 3:11). Then for the first time came those words that recur again and again throughout the Scriptures: "I will be with you" (3:12).

We read of the same reaction from Gideon in the Book of Judges, when the Israelites were being oppressed by the Midianites. Gideon, that timid and cautious young man, was beating out wheat in the underground wine press to hide it from the Midianites, when the angel of the Lord appeared and said to him, "The LORD is with you, you mighty warrior." And, as we might have done, Gideon protested, "But sir, if the LORD is with us, why then has all this happened to us? And where are all his wonderful deeds that our ancestors recounted to us? . . . But now the LORD has cast us off, and given us into the hand of Midian." But God brushed this aside. "Go," he said, "in this might of yours and deliver Israel from the hand of Midian; I hereby commission you." Gideon objected, "My clan is the weakest in Manasseh, and I am the least in my family." The Lord replied, "But I will be with you, and you shall strike down the Midianites, every one of them" (Judges 6:11-16).

"I will be with you." This is God's promise, and we must resolve to believe this promise and trust it, no matter what we have to endure. Freedom from pain and diminishment is not assured in this life—nor is any other thing here below— although we may earnestly pray for it. But of these we are certain: that God is with us, that his love encompasses us, and that those who persevere in this trust to the end will be saved and will come to him in peace in heaven. "Being with" us means that God enters into the suffering we have to bear on this earth. Christ was a refugee like so many victims of tyrannical governments: born in a stable, lacking comfort, on the run from Herod and narrowly escaping the fate of the slaughtered babies of Bethlehem, dying the death of a criminal and outcast.

In a number of the vivid stories of deliverance and healing in the Gospel of John, it is apparent that the initial response of the disciples is to grasp only the surface meaning of events. They interpret these events not in the way God intended but according to the accepted belief of their Jewish teachers. In the account of the man born blind (see John 9:1-41), the traditionally assumed reason for human afflictions—that they are God's punishment for sins—is demonstrated by the question the disciples put to Jesus. "Rabbi," they asked, "who sinned, this man or his parents, that he should have been born blind?" But Jesus answered, "Neither he nor his parents sinned. He was born blind so that God might be glorified in him" (9:2-3). As always, the disciples ask the wrong question.

We can hardly blame them, since we do the same in spite of all we have been taught. All too often, our initial response to the bad things that happen to us is, "What have I done to deserve this? God must be punishing me for my sins, holding my past wrongdoings against me, exacting compensation for the things I have done." This instinct seems to go back to the very beginnings of the human race, when, as Scripture says, our first parents chose to follow their own independent way instead of obeying their creator, and discovered what it was to have a guilty conscience. It almost seems as if God is now taking revenge on us for our disobedience. It is difficult to believe that God still loves us and is even now at work in this present trial, planning how to use it for our growth in understanding and compassion.

Looking to Scripture for Answers

Are we right to blame God when things go wrong, to reproach him for creating a universe in which conflicts are bound to occur and the innocent suffer? Railing against

Providence, demanding to know why, why, why God permits terrible things to happen to innocent, defenseless people, or attempting to justify God for allowing them—both reactions are equally foolish. We simply do not understand the mind of God. We may talk of tectonic plates in a constantly changing physical world, we may speak of the misuse of people's free will, but, in the last analysis, we have to turn to holy Scripture for the answer, or lack of answer, to our questions.

The Bible tackles this problem magnificently in the Book of Job, which makes use of an ancient folk story about God's testing the patience of a virtuous man with a series of calamities that all but overwhelm him. "In all this Job did not sin or charge God with wrongdoing" (Job 1:22). Finally, God acknowledges Job's steadfastness and restores all he had lost, adding even more blessings than he enjoyed before. Into this account the scriptural writer inserts an impassioned dialogue between Job and the friends who have come to sympathize with him. The friends insist on the conventional wisdom in defense of God's judgments: that Job has deserved his misfortunes through his own sins, for God rewards the virtuous and punishes the guilty. But Job insists on his innocence and demands justice from God. To and fro the argument goes without coming to any agreement, until at last the previously silent God puts a stop to it.

Answering out of a whirlwind, he shows that both positions are totally inadequate. Human understanding is altogether unequal to comprehending the ways of God, whose thoughts are infinitely above ours.

"Where were you when I laid the foundation of
the earth?
Who determined its measurements—surely
you know! . . .
Have you commanded the morning since your
days began,
and caused the dawn to know its place,
so that it might take hold of the skirts of the earth,
and the wicked be shaken out of it? . . .
Can you send forth lightnings, so that they may go
and say to you, 'Here we are'? . . .
Will you even put me in the wrong?
Will you condemn me that you may be justified?"
(Job 38:4-5, 12-13, 35; 40:8)

Relentlessly, the divine questions follow one another, show-ing the limitations of Job's knowledge—all expressed in some of the most sublime poetry ever written. Job acknowl-edges that he has spoken foolishly, and humbles himself before the Almighty. "I despise myself, and repent in dust and ashes." (42:6). In the epilogue, God condemns the friends for their ignorance and declares that Job has spoken better than they. Neither side is given the kind of answer they were hoping for, and neither are we (see 42:7-9).

Like Job, we want straight answers to our questions about the justice of God's decrees, and all we get is a poetic description of the marvels of his creation, a vision of world order that makes no sense because it is beyond the capacity of human reason. Suffering is part of this order, in which predator and prey occupy the same living space. God's world cannot be explained by logic, for God is beyond logic. Mystery is at the heart of existence. Even if we could grasp the meaning of it all, would that make us as wise as God, or would it bring God down to the level of our human minds? Would we then be satisfied? Discovering the kind of God who allows the innocent to suffer, the Book of Job evolves a new theology of suffering, a new concept of God: pain is the creative dimension of the divine artist. The reader is forced to ask whether it is more human to see suffering as deserved in some way, or whether it is the divine catalyst in the creation of some new aspect of eternal truth.[3]

For us, life is necessarily contingent; what gives it value is the way we react to it. So let us stop asking "Why me?" and begin to ask some different questions. "What does life mean for me?" Surely, at the deepest level, we are all searching for a meaningful existence. But what do we think *would* make life meaningful? What do we think life owes us? Is it happiness, appreciation of our gifts, the opportunity to fulfill our potential and our dreams, to find joy in our work and our relationships? To be understood and loved? Surely these are all valid answers. But are they the right questions? Do we regard these as things to which we are entitled, to which we can attain and hold on? When presented with such questions, most of us would respond, "Of course not."

In our wounded world, we cannot attain happiness and fulfillment by demanding and pursuing them. It is the saints who continually show us that we only achieve these things by giving them away, by seeking them for others. They are a by-product of our effort to give joy, love, and significance to other people's lives. The famous Prayer of St. Francis of Assisi expresses this unforgettably:

Lord, make me an instrument of your peace.
Where there is hatred, let me sow love;
where there is injury, let me sow pardon;
where there is discord, let me sow peace;
where there is error, let me bring truth;
where there is doubt, let me sow faith;
where there is despair, let me bring hope;
where there is darkness, let me bring light;
where there is sadness, let me bring joy.

O Divine Master, grant that I may not so much seek
to be consoled as to console;
to be understood as to understand;
to be loved as to love.
For it is in giving that we receive;
It is in forgiving that we are forgiven;
It is in dying that we are born to eternal life.

All the saints in their way say the same thing. What we should be seeking, says St. Francis de Sales, is not self-fulfillment but self-transcendence. St. Thérèse once said, "I felt charity enter my soul, and the need to forget myself and to please others; since then I've been happy!"[4]

To blame God for the suffering that comes upon us is to waste it, to fail the test and squander the opportunity to transcend our natural feelings. If we react to events with self-pity and complaining, we run the risk of blocking our awareness of God's goodness, and thus limiting our response. This could explain St. Benedict's abhorrence of "murmuring," and his strictures against brothers who obey with ill-will and murmur not only in words but in their hearts.

What Is God Asking of Me?

Christ, our leader in suffering, teaches us to turn outward to others rather than inward to self-pity. Instead of "What have I done to deserve this?" should we not affirm our faith in God's love and his power to turn everything to the good of those who believe in him and love him? (see Romans 8:28). Rather than asking the meaning of disasters and suffering, we should be questioning ourselves: "What is God asking of me in this situation? What is he hoping I will do with it? How can I respond to it and make it an act of faith and love?" As we saw earlier, God does not send suffering directly or inflict cruel punishment on us for our wrongdoing, but he does permit things to go wrong in this imperfect world in order to bring about a greater good. If our finite minds could understand this, remarked St. Francis de Sales, it would not say much for God's infinity.

St. Paul responds to these heart-searching questions in his Letter to the Colossians, where he tells the first Christians, "I am now rejoicing in my sufferings for your sake, and in my flesh I am completing what is lacking in Christ's afflictions for the sake of his body, that is, the church" (1:24). Paul was not saying that Christ's passion and death were insufficient for the world's redemption, but that in the limitations of his mortal body on earth he did not and could not undergo every kind of human suffering and diminishment. After all, Jesus did not, himself, experience blindness, deafness, or a particular disability during his earthly life. He was not born with an inherited disease; he had no mental or physical handicap; he never knew the weakness of old age. Neither did he experience what it was to be a woman, a married or divorced person, a single parent, an abused wife, or an abandoned child. All these things and many others he left to be embodied by his disciples in every generation. Each of us in our life can experience some of the things that were lacking in his. Because we have been incorporated into the body of Christ in baptism, we share the dying and rising of Jesus in our own particular time and circumstances; and so he continues his redeeming work in us until the end of time.

What dignity our Maker has bestowed upon his creatures that they should be allowed to play their part in the great work of redemption! When we think of this great privilege, our spirits are lifted up. It is not for the pain, the sickness, or the diminishment that we can rejoice, but because he is Lord in every situation and can turn all things to our good and to the building of his kingdom. He can incorporate our particular pain and suffering into his redeeming passion for the salvation of all. Paul sees his sufferings as contributing to that predetermined measure of tribulation that is the harbinger of the Parousia, the end of time when Christ will return in glory. He sees his suffering as a way of foreshortening this time of tribulation and hastening the time for the return of Christ in glory (see 2 Peter 3:12).

Tribulations borne in the name of Christ reduce the level of suffering to be endured by others for the purification of sin. Accepting pain cheerfully is not mere stoicism; it is a loving gift to our fellow men and women. Our pain has its ultimate origins in the rejection of God's friendship by the first human beings. Each subsequent generation is wounded and perpetuates its pain by inflicting it on others. Real Christian patience and steadfast endurance can halt this apparently inevitable transmission; instead of passing on the evil, patient endurance absorbs it so that the line of malice goes no further. As the saying goes, "The buck stops here." Acceptance of pain puts an end to the endless cycle of mutual hurt. This is what Christ did in his life on earth, and it is to this he calls us also—not to render evil for evil, but rather to bear patiently the hurt that is done to us.

Furthering Christ's Redeeming Work

One day I was talking with an elderly, blind clergyman about the instinctive reaction of so many people to suffering, "Why me? What have I done to deserve this?" After long thought, he said, "But, why not me? Perhaps God is asking something of me through this physical blindness that has come upon me. Perhaps if I embrace it wholeheartedly, not for itself, but because he has allowed it to happen, he can use this acceptance of mine to further his redeeming work; perhaps he needs my contribution. In any case, he knows what he is about." Man of God that he was, he had understood that it was not the blindness in itself that had the ability to further the redemption of the world, but his willing acceptance of what God had permitted.

While I was still thanking God for the wisdom of these words, another disabled friend came to stay for a few days at our guesthouse, to whom I related this conversation. "But, of course," she said at once, "why not me? Why shouldn't I accept my disability and have some share in our Lord's sufferings, when he died for me? Many people are far worse off than I am, but I can add my widow's mite." For her, it was an opportunity to be embraced. There are probably many more unknown and hidden sufferers who humbly and lovingly add their own small offering to the passion of Christ.

A gardening friend I met at the guesthouse found her peace in this truth. When she was quite young, her retina detached, resulting in severe loss of vision. How hard she had found it to accept the fact that she was now considered legally blind! There was so much she had hoped to be able to do. "At first," she told me, "I raged against it in total rebellion. But after a time, I realized that God was using my need to draw out depths of kindness and compassion in my family and friends that they never knew they possessed. And so I began to understand how we are all bound up together, members of the one body, and how the life of each one of us has its effect on all the others. Then I recognized my role."

A family living a few doors away from ours had a child with Down's syndrome. I used to see the little girl's parents or her fourteen-year-old brother taking her for daily walks, and I have never forgotten the loving patience they showed in their care and thoughtfulness for her. This family taught me that the disabled can exercise a kind of vicarious ministry to others, encouraging them to grow to a spiritual stature they might not otherwise attain.

Jean Vanier's stories of the L'Arche communities and the relationships between the mentally impaired members and the volunteer helpers illustrate this work of the Spirit over and over again. He tells of a severely disabled member of his community who was unable to walk, speak, or eat without assistance. He was very weak, constantly needing oxygen; yet, he was a ray of sunshine in the house. When anyone came up to him and called him by name, his eyes shone with loving trust and his face broke into a radiant

smile. Everyone liked to be near him, attracted by his little-
ness, his vulnerability, and his gentle beauty. He touched
and transformed the hearts of his helpers, showing them a
new dimension of being human. Through him they entered
a different world, a world not of action and competition,
but of contemplation, presence, and love. He did not ask
for money, power, or position; his basic need was for communication and love. It could be said that he revealed an
aspect of a God who does not remedy all our problems by
extraordinary power, but who appeals to our hearts and
calls them to communion.[5]

The mentally impaired seem to have an ability to trust
others and invite them to communion, which people who
are fully developed intellectually and physically have forgotten or rejected.[6] I once shared a hospital room with a
developmentally disabled young woman who had a mental
age of about six. She lived in a hostel with other girls, earn-
ing a little money by making cotton wool swabs. At first
shy and a little frightened by her hospital surroundings, she
began to respond in trust to the nurses and other patients,
offering to lend them the comic books she bought at the
magazine cart, and smiling happily when the other patients
chatted with her. We all found our hearts strangely moved
and warmed by her confidence in us.

The truth is that people with mental disabilities have a
unique role in the breaking down of barriers that separate
people and prevent their living happy lives. While the world
is trapped in unending competition and the search for suc-

cess, this concern does not exist for the disabled and mentally impaired. What is important for them is affection and relationships. For normal people with their busy schedules, engaging in relationships with the mentally or physically disabled can be time consuming, demanding, and stressful. We can fear being swallowed up by such relationships. But it is not so for the mentally impaired—they are utterly defenseless, needing care, needing to be loved and accepted. Jean Vanier said of them, "In order for them to live, to be fulfilled, they need relationships. They need communion more than generosity. The particular gift of the disabled is to lead others into communion."[7] Perhaps only after death will they see what they have unknowingly done for others—drawing out gifts of compassion and joy and providing a model of living in and celebrating the present moment.

People have gained maturity and grown in love and generosity through caring for a disabled child or relative. The transforming effect of adversity can be seen in the story of a businessman whose wife developed a mental illness and became progressively unable to look after herself. She was a shadow of what she had once been; she could neither feed, wash, nor dress herself without help. Her husband had always been a strong personality, efficient, well organized, domineering, and exacting. He had far too much to do to waste time listening to other people. His employees feared him and his family dreaded his wrath. Yet, somehow he could not bring himself to have his wife hospitalized. Against all expectations, he became the one who washed and fed her, brushed her teeth, and helped her to get dressed. Still efficient and capable, he began to develop a side of himself that neither he nor anyone else knew existed. It revealed itself in a gentle love for a defenseless person, a capacity for listening and understanding, a delicacy of touch, and a tone of voice that showed his wife that he still regarded her as important and as someone he valued. With his firm, yet gentle, hands and the expression of his eyes, his attitude was wholly reassuring.

She had somehow touched in him the hidden depths of his being, drawing out of him gifts of love, compassion, and goodness that he had never permitted to emerge before. Her need, her trust in her husband, gradually enabled a real communion of spirit to develop between them. She had awakened his heart and helped him to admit that he did not always have to be the boss, the strong, successful person who made others feel inferior. It was acceptable to have his own weaknesses; there was no need to wear a mask and appear to be other than he was. He could be himself. Through discovering the hidden qualities of his sick wife, the husband began to discover acceptability in his own lack of perfection and to realize that vulnerability can be a privileged and beautiful place of communion, the place of God's presence. The weak need the strong, but inner healing is brought about when the strong discover their need for the weak—whose special gift is the ability to lead people into communion.[8]

Witnessing to the Value of Human Life

"The courage and the serenity with which so many of our brothers and sisters suffering from serious disabilities lead their lives when they are shown acceptance and love bears eloquent witness to what gives authentic value to life, and makes it, even in difficult conditions, something precious for them and for others," wrote Pope John Paul II.[9] In his last years, he himself was a prophetic figure for the value and dignity of human life, bearing his disabilities steadfastly and continuing to fulfill his teaching ministry in every way still open to him. In this he was a powerful sign against abortion, euthanasia, genocide, and "designer" babies. John Paul II showed that a disabled person can be a prophet to our time, speaking with his very disabilities of the unique value of his life. During his visit to Slovakia in 2003, where his weakness was very evident, he wanted to show that someone with physical limitations could still be a useful member of society. By not trying to hide his illness, he became a living example of Christlike courage, and in his dying he was still teaching the world how to go to God as one full of hope and trust.

The place for those with a severe mental disability in the body of Christ is simply to be the presence, the icon, the sacrament of Jesus in his passion. They have no voice, but they are temples of the Holy Spirit; their unique role is to be his beloved child, a home for Jesus and his Father, a secret living tabernacle for God.

Victims of Alzheimer's disease, whose degeneration causes such distress to their families, are still persons with their own unique gifts to offer, no matter how diminished they seem. Who knows what God is secretly working out in their souls? A sister in our community developed this dreaded disease in her mid-fifties. She needed constant reassurance to her questions: "What is happening? What am I supposed to do? Where should I be?" Eventually, to our great sorrow, we had to arrange for her to live in a nursing home, where she could receive the kind of care that had become beyond our skills, in spite of our love for her. She could no longer express herself or engage in conversation. The one thing that brought her fleeting happiness was for us to sing with her—sometimes old songs, but most often the plainchant of the Daily Office she had known so well. She never tired of singing the opening phrases of the *Salve Regina,* which, as chantress in the monastic choir, she had regularly intoned. It was said that she could recall these melodies because musical elements are stored in a different part of the brain from verbal memories, and so we would encourage her to join in whatever we were singing. Sometimes the other patients took part and found a momentary companionship. Although she remained as sweet and gentle as she had always been, occasionally when we visited her we would find tears running down her cheeks, indicating a suffering and frustration she could not express.

However, it is well known that not all Alzheimer's patients are always sweet and gentle. One of the most distressing aspects of the disease is that a patient sometimes seems to suffer a personality change, becoming very aggressive and hard to reach. It is difficult for families and friends to believe this is the same person they had lived with in the past. Yet, in such cases, the inner core of the person is untouched and precious in the sight of God. It seems as if he has hidden the person away in his own secret place where he can perfect his refining and healing work, and only in the next life shall we see the beauty and purpose of it, and understand that even when mentally impaired, confused, and frustrated, a person is still an "immortal diamond."[10] As children, we were taught to have great respect for those with a mental disability because such people were wholly innocent, unable to commit a deliberate sin with full knowledge and understanding, and therefore they were especially beautiful in God's eyes. This belief was more widespread in medieval times than it is now, but I believe that it still forms a part of traditional Russian spirituality, which sees life in terms of the battle between good and evil. In any case it is still valid.

In the Book of Genesis, Abraham pleads with the Lord not to destroy the city of Sodom because of the wickedness of its citizens (see Genesis 18:16-33). This account has always appeared to me as a paradigm of the role of the poor, diminished, and insignificant of this world. People usually see in this story the importance of hospitality, intercession, and persevering prayer, and indeed this is the immediate message. However, the passage contains an equally important element: the Lord promises to spare the city if he can find fifty just and upright people in it. Through persistent bargaining, Abraham succeeds in whittling the number down to ten. Apparently even this small number cannot be found, and the Lord rains down fire and brimstone on Sodom, destroying it entirely—though for Abraham's sake, he does allow his nephew Lot and his family to make their escape.

In this passage, the old, the sick, and the infirm of the world are shown their all-important task. They are meant to be the ten just and upright people for whom the Lord will spare our sinful society. The prophet Jeremiah even reduces the number to one when he says:

> Run to and fro through the streets of Jerusalem,
>   look around and take note!
> Search its squares and see
>   if you can find one person
> who acts justly
>   and seeks truth—
> so that I may pardon Jerusalem.
> (Jeremiah 5:1)

Surely each of us can find here a word for ourselves. Can I be that one person trying to do what is right and seek the truth? Can we infirm and diminished people together raise that number to ten, twenty, thirty, forty, even fifty?

Chapter 8

We are living in an increasingly secularized society. Many churches and communities see their numbers dwindling, and we often ask ourselves what we are doing wrong to cause this lack of growth. We are probably no more slack than the communities of former times. Young people today not only have more options to choose from, but the surrounding philosophy of life is one of moral and doctrinal relativism. There is no clear sense of right and wrong—you may do what you like so long as it makes you happy—and neither is there any such thing as absolute truth. In such a climate, it is hard for young people to commit themselves to anything. However, even if a community seems to be dying out, its members are still individually called by God to be faithful to their vocation, for God never repents of his gifts. People may grow old and frail, but they still have their task in this world, and who knows if they may be the ones to save the rest of society and renew its vision? We need the great saints for their prophetic character and inspiring example, but we also need the little, hidden saints to save the world.

Freedom to Choose How to Respond

We cannot change our lot in this life, but we can change our attitude toward it. Everything can be taken from us except the last of our human freedoms: to choose how to respond to circumstances. It may be our task to suffer; no one can suffer in our place. Our opportunity lies in how we embrace our task, and this is what gives meaning to our life. It has been said that people can endure anything if they see a meaning in it. The meaning for us is by our willing acceptance to increase the amount of love in the world, and so help to build up God's kingdom. In accepting the challenge to suffer bravely, our life has meaning until its last moment.[11]

We have not, of course, come to the end of accepting trials and diminishments. Throughout life there will be continual little deaths and relinquishments. At these times, it is often difficult to keep our spirits fixed on the risen life to which we are called in Christ, when the flesh exerts its downward pull and our mental resources are low. It might even seem as if God expects too much of us poor creatures—who alone of all living things (as far as we know) are a combination of both matter and spirit.

Keeping body and spirit in harmony amid the vicissitudes of life is a constant struggle that can sometimes seem beyond our strength. But that is the very reason why the Father sent his Son to become one of us, and to share our twofold nature of body and spirit. It is also why Jesus gave the sacraments to his people—those simple but powerful tangible signs that contain a material element capable of being grasped by our senses, as well as an inward grace that we lay hold of by faith. In scholastic language, they are signs that effect what they signify. These helps were not given to angels or animals, but only, in the Lord's tender compassion, to us human beings.

At every stage of our lives, we are offered an accompanying sacrament—baptism with water for new birth in Christ, sealing with chrism to confirm and strengthen this new life, the bread and wine of the Eucharist to nourish it, confession of sin and words of forgiveness to reconcile us to God and his church, the anointing of the sick in old age or terminal illness, when our journey through life is nearing its end.

What in fact is God's plan for our life? Are we so absorbed in our pain and struggles, so afraid of what further diminishment God is going to burden us with, that we see everything from our own perspective rather than his? God's plan for us cannot be only more and more pain. His love for us is so great that he is incapable of thinking in negative terms, in plans of diminishment rather than growth. Our destiny is rather something creative, original, thrilling. Ultimately, his will for us all is that we be united with him in heaven, where no eye has seen, nor ear heard, nor the human heart conceived, what God has prepared for those who love him (see 1 Corinthians 2:9). But on the way there, our task must be to grow deeper and deeper in faith and love, and to extend his kingdom on earth *through* these challenges, not in spite of them.

1. Cardinal Joseph Bernardin, *Journey to Peace* (New York: Doubleday, 1996).

2. John Henry Newman, *Meditations on Christian Doctrine,*

March 7, 1848, 2, http://www.newmanreader.org/works/meditations/meditations9.html.

3. Dermot Cox, *Man's Anger and God's Silence: The Book of Job* (Slough, UK: St. Paul's Publications, 1950).

4. Thérèse of Lisieux, Story of a Soul, trans. John Clarke (Washington: ICS Publications, 1976), 99.

5. Jean Vanier, *Tout Personne est une Histoire Sacrée* (Paris: Plon, 1994).

6. Jean Vanier, p. 250.

7. Jean Vanier, p. 249.

8. Jean Vanier, p. 249.

9. Pope John Paul II, *Evangelium vitae* (On the Value and Inviolability of Human Life), March 25, 1995, 63.

10. Gerard Manley Hopkins, "That Nature is a Heraclitean Fire and of the Comfort of the Resurrection," http://www.bartleby.com/122/48.html.

11. Victor Frankl, *Man's Search for Meaning* (Boston: Beacon Press, 2006).

Acknowledgments

I would like to give thanks for the support and encouragement of my abbess and community during the time of writing this book, and to mention especially Dame Petra Boex, who read each chapter carefully as it surfaced, and Dame Maria Boulding, who scrutinized it with a theologian's eye and caught lurking typographical mistakes before they could get into print. I am also grateful for the encouragement of Abbot Richard Yeo, Abbess Máire Hickey, Abbot Paul Stonham, Dom Alan Rees, Dom Stephen Ortiger, and all our Stanbrook Oblates, as well as for the continuing interest and support of Fr. Hugh Sinclair, Fr. Joseph di Mauro, and Sr. Patricia Mary England. I also want to thank my many disabled friends who have been such an inspiration to me; some of them I never knew by name. My thanks also to Patricia Mitchell of The Word Among Us Press, who has steered the book on its course and made my British English expressions more intelligible to American readers.